Savour of Scotland

*A photographic and gastronomic
tour of Scotland a century ago*

George Morrison

Period photographs and recipes specially prepared by the Author

LINDSAY PUBLICATIONS

First published 1997 by Lindsay Publications, Glasgow

ISBN 1 898169 12 8

©1997 George Morrison

*This book is dedicated to Joan Fitzpatrick
in grateful appreciation of her many kindnesses*

The moral right of the author has been asserted

All rights reserved

No part of this publication may be reproduced, stored in a retrieval system, or transmitted in any form, or by any means, electronic, mechanical, photocopying, recording or otherwise, without the express written permission of the publisher.

British Library Cataloguing-in-Publication Data
A Catalogue record for this book is available from the British Library

Designed by Mitchell Graphics, Glasgow

Printed and bound in Great Britain by Redwood Books

ACKNOWLEDGEMENTS

Among the many who have given generously of their help and advice in the preparation of this book I would especially like to acknowledge that of the late Dr I F Grant, whose books, so carefully researched and documented, are an invaluable source of information on Scottish folk life. She not only provided essential information, but gave me access to her unique collection of photographs and was kind enough to explain much detail in them that might otherwise have been unclear to me. Great assistance was given to me also by Dr O'Brien of the Glasgow City Archive of the Mitchell Library, whose encyclopaedic knowledge of the disparate visual material in her care rendered my task not only much easier but more agreeable. I am indebted also to the kindness of the late Dr Charles McDonogh, who provided me with many photographs of interest. The Central Public Library of Aberdeen, The Central Public Library of Edinburgh, Dundee Public Library, The National Monuments Record of Scotland, and Mrs John Greenhow have been of great assistance, as has Mr Robin Gard of the Northumbria Record Office. The remaining visual material was most kindly placed at my disposal by a donor who desires to remain anonymous.

Lastly, I should like to acknowledge, in remembrance, the great help given me by my late wife and the important information on Scottish food to be found among the entries in her gastronomical encyclopaedia *The Food of the Western World*.

The sources of the photographs and their page references are as follows:-

Copyright: Central Public Library, Aberdeen,
  pages 68, 89, 103 and 111.
Copyright: Central Public Library, Edinburgh,
  pages 118, 120 and 122.
Copyright: Dundee Public Library,
  page 114.
Copyright: Glasgow City Archives, The Mitchell Library, Glasgow,
  pages 13, 15, 17, 19, 20, 23, 27, 28, 35, 37, 39, 40, 43, 55, 57, 58, 61, 62, 64, 67, 73 and 75.
Dr I F Grant,
  pages 46, 49, 51, 52, 70, 78, 80, 82, 85, 87, 95 and 96.
Copyright: Mrs John Greenhow
  page 25.
Dr Charles McDonogh,
  pages 31, 32, 44, 101, 104, 106 and 109.
Copyright: The National Monuments Record of Scotland,
  pages 99 and 117.
Copyright: The National Museum of Antiquities of Scotland,
  page 76
Copyright: The Northumberland Record Office,
  page 125.
Private Collection,
  pages 6, 9, 10, 44, 89 and 90.

INTRODUCTION

What is the secret of the magic in the name, Scotland? The many strands that go to make up the texture of Scotland and its people are interwoven as closely as a splendid Harris tweed, as colourfully as a tartan. The mysterious Picts, the Scotae with their Celtic background, the Romans, the Norsemen, the Auld Alliance; all deployed upon a diversified territory shaped by an ocean warmed by the Gulf Stream. It is a land of romance that has drawn travellers from abroad for centuries.

The survival of the Clan system of social organisation into comparatively recent times has meant that the influence of medieval social patterns in the Highlands has been greatly diluted. The relative absence of State feudalism allows us, even today, to experience something of the atmosphere of an earlier time. One cannot do better than first to read the works of some of Scotland's great writers, such as Robert Burns, Sir Walter Scott and Robert Louis Stephenson, particularly the first and the last for their wonderful sensitivities to the liveliness of local speech.

Thrawn Janet, by Robert Louis Stevenson, must surely be regarded as one of the most brilliant uses of dialect to achieve atmosphere to be found in the literature of Europe's off-shore islands, as well as one of the best creepy stories ever written.

The visitor to Scotland should first gather the impressions of those who visited Scotland in the past, such as Boswell and Johnson. Photographs, too play an important part in revealing the savour of Scotland's past – as well as its present.

Until the middle of the last century, a trip to and around Scotland was a serious undertaking. It took a week to get from London to Edinburgh – longer if the weather was bad. Brief stops in the middle of each day to cram down tough boiled beef in fifteen minutes and be jolted into hours of indigestion can have been no fun, though, if one was unable to secure an inside seat, exposure to the weather must have acted as a powerful counter-irritant. At the end of each day, the prospect of uncertain accommodation would have been mitigated only by the effects of excessive fatigue. The presence of agitated and possibly travel-sick children in the confined interior of a stage-coach? Suffice it to say that our pre-railway travellers had need of both determination and forbearance.

It is hardly surprising that some chose to travel by sea, though the delays due to weather could be worse than those encountered by land. When both categories of travellers arrived, they found that Thomas Telford's network of nearly a thousand miles of roadways in Scotland, suitable for stage-coaches, did not give adequate access to many of the places that today are regarded as the most worth seeing..

It was the coming of the steam-ship, the opening of the through connection by rail between London and Edinburgh and Glasgow and the growth of the Scottish railway system that enabled an increasing tourist traffic to appear and to feed, in its turn, the growth of hotels. By the 1880s Scotland had become widely accessible and the way was opened for the development of the grouse moors on a commercial scale. These changes disrupted many lives. The changes in the Highlands brought about by the enclosures and the commercialisation of sheep farming by the introduction of the large sheep-walks, reliant on distant markets, had already undermined the stability of the old ways and too great a dependence on the potato had also created havoc, though not on the same disastrous scale as in Ireland.

The changing marketing structures and the commercialisation

of the grouse moors, together with the development of the steam-trawler and the rail transportation of fish in bulk paved the way for the 'Highlands and Islands' to become a depressed area and led to the setting up of the Congested Districts Board, a palliative measure also tried in Ireland.

Unlike Ireland however, the structure of the Scottish clans had given a unique social and cultural flavour to Scottish life, which remains strongly felt even to this day, and is one of the stimulating components of the Scots character..

Another important difference between Scotland and Ireland is that Ireland has no large islands off its shores. The largest ones have only with great difficulty remained inhabited while Scotland has islands of such extent that stable communities have been more effectively maintained upon them.

The island communities, in many cases separated from one another and from the mainland by large stretches of water, have led to another characterising feature of Scottish life, the growth of elaborate ferry services and a heightened appreciation of the importance of the sea as a communications medium which has helped to give Scotland her great maritime tradition.

It is the differences between countries that make travel really interesting and we can imagine the excitement that would have filled a group of travellers taking their places in the train about to leave from Kings Cross or Euston stations a century ago. Nowadays when so many travellers drive their own cars, the transition from England to Scotland is a more gradual one and the attention of the driver, at least, is distracted by the cares of driving. Travelling by train, however, one can observe, not only the changing scene beyond the windows but such things as the way in which the flavour of the food in the restaurant car changes. By far the most delightful way of approaching the west of Scotland is by sea, though this route is, unhappily, no longer available to the average traveller.

Travel sharpens our sense of living. It is the best tonic in the world. As we visit Scotland today, let us look at what travellers a century ago would have found unrolling before them, especially those who would have come by sea, for no better introduction can be had to that great centre of Scottish life: Glasgow.

On the main deck of a steamer heading from London to Glasgow, C. 1900

By far the most picturesque and adventurous way of travelling to Scotland available to our prospective party of tourists from London would have been to take the direct sea passage, London to Glasgow, entailing a voyage along the south coast of England, past the Isle of Wight, past Plymouth and Falmouth, the Lizard and Land's End, then up the St George's Channel, the Irish Sea, past the Isle of Man, through the North Channel and so into the Firth of Clyde. This journey would have taken three days. Of all the ways of approaching Scotland this was the most romantic, with wonderful views of hills and water as the Firth of Clyde gradually closed about the vessel and the indications of Glasgow's maritime life became ever more apparent until the moment of their arrival at Springfield Quay in the very heart of the city.

This route was chiefly operated by the Clyde Shipping Company, who ran mixed cargo and passenger vessels. The company had begun life as steam-tug owners on the Clyde as far back as 1815, only three years after Bell's *Comet* had gone into service, but entered the coastal passenger trade in 1856. The number of cabins available on the company's ships would have suited a small group, so that travelling together in this way would have seemed almost like sailing on their own private steam-yacht; nothing but congenial company aboard.

The service was interrupted by the two World Wars and did not continue long after the second, but the company still survives and operates today as Clyde-based tug-owners.

The author remembers with great pleasure making this journey as a boy. The whole atmosphere was informal, one had the run of the ship, from the bridge to the engine-room, where, under the watchful but friendly eye of the chief engineer one could appreciate that astonishingly beautiful piece of mechanism the compound, triple-expansion, marine steam-engine. While one's appetite, given the keenest of edges by the sea air, was regularly satisfied by excellent meals. Sea-water baths only were available on board, in which the soap refused to lather. These were heated in an unusual way. The bath was filled from a single cold sea-water tap to the required height and a valve was then opened which allowed steam to enter the water through a series of tiny holes, very quickly raising the temperature of the sea-water to the desired point.

It seems a great shame that this delightful way of journeying over the sea has been swept away and, in its place, we are given the alternative of sitting strapped into a baby's chair in a crowded bus above the clouds. A most unsociable way of travelling, however expeditious.

A Glasgow-bound steamer setting out from Belfast, C. 1900.

TRAVELLERS FROM IRELAND HAD, IN THE NINETEENTH CENTURY, a variety of sea routes to Glasgow from many of the larger Irish ports, such as Dublin, Cork, Limerick, Londonderry and Wexford, but that chiefly used was from Belfast. The two cities had much in common and both were centres of the large ship-building industry. A community of interest, both religious and industrial linked the two cities as they still do today. The Scottish ship-owners G and J Burns and the Belfast Steamship Company ran regular services across the North Channel and the Irish Sea. Like the Clyde, the Lagan river had, over the years, been deepened by the building of training walls and by dredging, to the extent that the biggest vessels afloat in the 1890s and in the early years of the twentieth century, vessels such as the *Oceanic* and later, the *Titanic* built by Harland and Wolff's shipyard, could be launched safely into the river. The passage through the North Channel and up the Firth of Clyde was an overnight one and those with maritime interests and who arose early enough could enjoy the fascinating experience of encountering vessels of all kinds as the Firth narrowed in between its hills and the shipping became confined to the river channel. In the summer an early breakfast was well worthwhile if ship-spotting happened to be among one's interests. Super excellent grilled Loch Fyne kippers were a feature of the menu and they are still widely to be had today. Here is a different way of enjoying them which takes a few days to prepare but is so delicious that one feels amply rewarded for the small amount of trouble.

Loch Fyne Kippers with Lemon-juice and Demerara Sugar.

Take as many Loch Fyne kippers as may be needed. Lay them on a dish that will fit into the refrigerator. Spread the kippers in a single layer on the dish, skin side down. Sprinkle their upper surfaces liberally with lemon juice and lightly with demerara sugar and rub this in with the fingertips. Put them into the refrigerator (not the freezer) and leave them until the next day. Next day rub them lightly with a little olive oil. The following day repeat the first operation, but be sparing with the demerara. On the fourth day repeat the olive oil and on the fifth day remove the backbones, sprinkle with lemon juice only, slice them thinly as you would smoked salmon and serve them just as they are with freshly baked wholemeal bread and butter.

The Prince of Wales' yacht Britannia *sailing down the Firth of Clyde, 1893.*

As dawn freshened and the steamer glided, in sheltered water, past the hills of the Firth of Clyde, those lucky enough to travel at the right time could have enjoyed a magnificent and memorable sight, the stately progress of one of the greatest of the great racing yachts of the 1890s, The Prince of Wales' *Brittania*, built in 1893, with a spread of canvas of over 1000 square metres. In the five years following her launch she won an incredible total of one hundred and twenty-two races. 1893 was also the year when several of the large yachts crossed the Atlantic in both directions to compete in one another's waters, a tradition which has continued to this day. The great cutter-rigged yacht was typical of a period of construction when the great yachts were still ships, before the relentless competition for speed had generated the sea-skimmers of later years which followed an evolutionary trend that now condemns the crews of racing yachts to genuine discomfort. These great cutters were an exception to the witty American Navy saying:

> *Those who go down to the sea in ships see*
> *the works of the Lord,*
> *But those who go down to the sea in cutters*
> *see Hell!*

This observation applied particularly to the small cutters used by the US Revenue Service, aboard which living conditions were said to be tough indeed. The great racing cutters of the 1890s and the early years of the twentieth century were very different, with luxurious accommodation for their owners and officers. Even the crew's quarters were more roomy than on the biggest racing yachts of the largest class today. Numbered among their crew were chefs and stewards and even, in some cases, a sea-going butler! Such vessels were capable of being used for pleasure cruising, for the relentless pressures which led to the specialised differentiation of present day categories were only beginning to be felt and indeed, at the time, were even resisted by the Yacht Racing Association, for sailing was then regarded as an amateur, recreative enjoyment, not as a frenzied competition between industrial sponsors as it tends to be now. So much late twentieth-century sport has become an industrial publicity device to capture potential markets through influencing the passive viewers of 'the goggle-box'.

When these great yachts were not engaged in racing, they could be and often were used by their owners, to bring parties of guests on extended cruises. The West Coast of Scotland provided a unique cruising ground of both sheltered and more open waters, diversified as it still is today by scenery as fine as may be found anywhere in the world. How lucky were those guests, for they were enjoying a pleasure which, in only two decades, would be gone forever, together with those great silent white leviathans themselves.

A lady guest aboard one of the great yachts of the 1890s

Here we enter a region of elegance and style that has quite passed away. To go cruising aboard one of these silent giants through the diverse enchantments of the Western Isles, with the best of company, the best of food and, best of all, no pressures of time or duty to compel a scheduled return after a brief spell of freedom. Such pleasures are hardly to be had in the final years of the twentieth century, nor could they easily be revived, for the great cutter-rigged yachts themselves have gone and the few schooners that remain are fitted with auxiliary internal-combustion engines.

Under the influence of Dixon Kemp, the 'plank-on-edge' concept of racing-yacht design had been abandoned and the increase in beam afforded space for relatively roomy salons in which the art of gastronomy could be enjoyed. What more fitting dish than a properly prepared cold *Homaris homaris*. Here is my family's method of preparing cold lobster.

Lobster Morrison

1 large lobster, freshly cooked in sea-water and allowed to grow cold in the water
500ml classically made mayonnaise, in which lemon juice replaces vinegar

Disarticulate the fore-legs and their claws, saving the juices and remove the 'thumbs' from the claws. Remove the shell by clipping with a pair of electrical side-cutters, carefully extracting the claw meat intact and reserving in a bowl all the juices from within the shell, so that the extracted meat can be put into this juice and kept moist. Reserve in another bowl the whitish curd that can be scraped off the interior of the shell segments with a small spoon, keeping it moist.

Detach the tail intact by gently but firmly pulling it away from the head end with slight sideways bending movements. By clipping both top and bottom of the tail shell segments the entire tail can be removed whole and the alimentary canal pulled out. Split the body by turning it legs uppermost and, laying the blade of a sharp strong knife along the centre-line, hit the back of the blade with a wooden mallet. If internal coral is present, pound it in a mortar and beat it into the mayonnaise, together with the creamy curd from the interior surface of the shell, if external coral is present in a hen fish, just beat this into the mayonnaise directly, without pounding. Be sure to include the soft, greenish liver, which contributes a particularly fine flavour to the sauce. Lay leaves of lettuce on a serving dish and arrange the lobster meat attractively on them. Pour half of the lobster juice over the flesh and beat the remainder into the mayonnaise with the curd, liver and coral which will give a delicious and digestible sauce to be served in a sauce-boat.

H.M.S. Agamemnon *and the Imperial Russian Navy cruiser* Rurik *fitting-out on the Clyde, 1906*

IF OUR TRAVELLERS HAD BEEN MAKING THEIR APPROACH UP THE Clyde on a morning in 1906, they might have seen an unusual sight, H.M.S. *Agamemnon*, one of the Royal Navy's last pre-Dreadnought type capital ships, berthed beside the Imperial Russian Navy's cruiser *Rurik* in Beardmore's fitting out basin.

H.M.S. *Agamemnon* and her sister ship the *Royal Sovereign* were the last battleships to be built before Lord Fisher's battleship design policy was put into effect and, though launched several years previously, she was still apparently being fitted out by her builders, Beardmore and Company. But the real puzzle of the photograph is the *Rurik*. Why is she berthed at Beardmore's? She was built by Vickers-Armstrong at Barrow on Furness, to the south of the Solway Firth, and launched in 1906, so what brings her here to Beardmore's on the Clyde? It looks as though she is awaiting her turn to avail of the exceptionally large Titan crane. *Rurik*, named after the founder of the Russian royal dynasty, though a smaller vessel, had considerably more powerful engines than *Agamemnon* and could make 21½ knots as against *Agamemnon*'s 16½ at top speed. Besides her secondary armament, she carried four 10 inch wire-wound marine rifles. The *Agamemnon*'s principle armament consisted of similar guns but of 12 inch bore. Perhaps the *Rurik*'s extended fitting out may have saved her from being dispatched with Admiral Rozdezsvenky's doomed fleet, drawn from the Baltic Squadron, which sailed two-thirds of the way around the world, overcoming immense logistical difficulties, to be almost completely destroyed or captured by the Japanese in the Straits of Tsushima, thus saving *Rurik* for her distinguished service in the Baltic during the early years of World War I, when, though not one of the chief vessels engaged, she acted as one of the supporting ships in the action, by which the Imperial Russian Navy obtained the Imperial German Navy's code books from a German warship by forcing the vessel to run herself aground and capturing it.

The *Rurik*, like other cruisers based at Kronstadt, in the Gulf of Riga, played its part in the 1917 Revolution, though not as prominently as the older cruiser *Aurora*, which sailed up the Neva, bombarded the fortress of Saints Peter and Paul and sent parties ashore to occupy the bridges across the Neva.

H.M.S. *Agamemnon*, though essentially regarded as old-fashioned after Lord Fisher's reforms, was called upon to take part in the covering bombardment for the Dardanelles landings in 1915, to relieve the pressure on other capital ships of more modern construction which were so badly needed for other duties at the time. The presence of these two vessels, together, indicates how much work for the British Admiralty and how much for other navies was carried out by shipyards on the Clyde.

The Drawing Office, Beardmore and Company's Shipbuilding Yard on the Clyde, C. 1905

THEN AS NOW, CONSTRUCTION OF A GREAT SHIP BEGINS IN THE mind of a marine architect who is also an engineer. Today this mental concept first finds actualisation in a computer model, which can be tested in its performance by subjecting it to programmes simulating the stresses that the proposed vessel would have to encounter on the high seas. In the days before computers, these ideas were first transferred to paper in the drawing offices of the great shipyards, many of which had their installations on the River Clyde because of the exceptionally ample sheltered waters which that great artery of Scottish life provided. At around this period it was not uncommon for more than half the tonnage of ships built in the United Kingdom to be built on the Clyde.

As computer simulation was not available, actual scale models were made and tested and the results incorporated in changes to the design, requiring changes in the drawings.

As the innumerable details of that vast undertaking which is the construction of a ship were planned, drawings of ever increasing detail were required – drawings which, in the later stages of design, showed every frame, every stanchion, every plate and, before the introduction of welding, every rivet-hole, running sometimes into six figure numbers. All these infinitely detailed drawings and tracings had to be prepared by a staff of marine draughtsmen whom we see at work at their trestle tables in the early years of this century. Such a huge number of drawings and tracings needed an elaborate, secure filing system and a little of this is to be seen at the left of the photograph where the filing cabinets for the large drawings and tracings can be seen. All this work needed good light and one wall of the drawing-office consists of windows, but daylight could not possibly have provided a sufficient amount of working time, particularly in the winter, so a row of automatically feeding electric arc lamps are suspended from the roof-truss. On major urgent projects, staff worked around the clock, on a shift basis, to keep construction going continuously in the yard. Paper was cheap but steel and labour were expensive commodities, so all the calculations and the meticulous drawings were checked and double-checked before being sent down, as tracings, to the different departments of the shipyard where the actual construction was put in hand. Electric arc lighting had only been introduced in the early 1880s and the serious effects of ultra-violet light from these sources on the retina were hardly yet appreciated but, with the lighting arrangements seen here, draughtsmen on night shifts must have felt their effects after a comparatively short time.

The Plating Shed, Beardmore and Company's Shipbuilding Yard on the Clyde, C. 1905

From the drawing office the drawings and tracings went to the mould-makers, the foundries, the sheds where the steel for the frame was prepared and to the plating-shed, where the steel plates, which formed the vessel's watertight skin, were marked, cut, punched, drilled and shaped, each to conform in three dimensions to its exact positioning on the steel frame of the hull. The first operation was to transfer the markings on the tracings from the drawing office onto the stock steel plating bought in by the shipbuilders. In the foreground of this photograph two men and a boy are engaged in this task. Each plate is then cut, according to the markings, to its appropriate size and configuration and then, in huge hydraulic presses, just visible in the background, bent to give it the exact shape to fit in its place on the ship's steel frame so that, when riveted into position, a perfect fit would result. These steel plates, which in the case of the armour-plate used in warship construction could weigh many tons, required elaborate handling equipment such as the hoists, derricks and cables seen throughout the plating shop. A large power-punch is seen to the right and, in the right background the powerful hydraulic presses for giving the plates their correct curvature.

At the time of this photograph, before the introduction of welding techniques of construction, the steel members of the keel and frame were riveted together with hundreds of thousands of rivets and the plating riveted to the frame and each plate to those beside, above and below it, thus forming an overlapping watertight seal. At first this was done by two men with sledge-hammers working on either side of the plate, then, in the 1890s, hydraulic riveting-machines were introduced, which squeezed the white-hot rivets into place, but, at about the time this photograph was taken, the pneumatic riveting-machines were coming in. Welding has now replaced almost all the use of riveting in shipbuilding. A memorable sight in the days of riveting was the succession of white-hot rivets, being thrown from the brazier where they were heated, across perhaps twelve or fifteen feet and being caught in tongs by the men who were inserting them in the rivet-holes. Steaming up the Clyde at night this was to be seen at all the active shipyards. Smoking was discouraged in the shipyards, not for health reasons as it is today, but because it was felt that it resulted in loss of productive time and though cigarette smoking was tolerated, the smoking of pipes often led to pipe-smokers not being engaged on account of the time required to prepare and fill a pipe and the fact that one hand was often in use holding it!

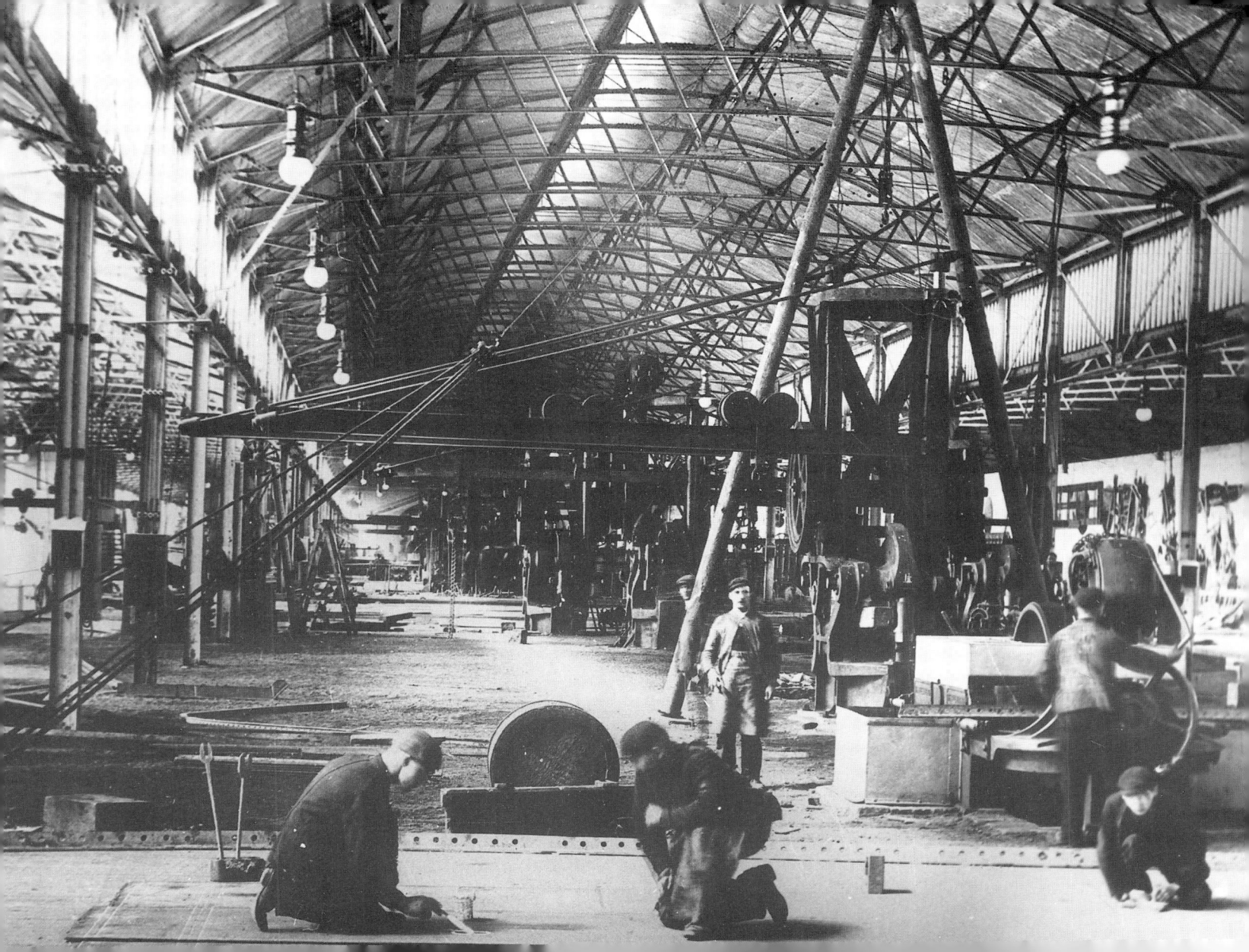

A coaling barge coaling a liner, Glasgow, C. 1890

As our overseas visitors approached their landing place, they would have been likely to see a sight which, though they might not have realised it, epitomised the concourse of resources that made Glasgow the great port that it still is today. The Clyde, coal and iron ore. It was the close physical juxtaposition of these three that made it possible for the astute Scottish entrepreneurs of the nineteenth century to set in train events which resulted in the growth of one of the mightiest shipbuilding centres in the world: a maritime city where some of the greatest liners ever built had their origin and a centre of marine engineering paralleled by few others. On a number of years a greater tonnage of ships was built here than anywhere else in the United Kingdom. Scotland had a reputation for excellence in shipbuilding going right back to the thirteenth century, perhaps a legacy from those great early marine designers the Vikings, whose hull forms are still admired by marine architects, for it was the port of Inverness to which, in the year 1242, a powerful French Baron went to have a ship built which would be large enough to carry himself and his vassals to Palestine. The hugely increasing demand for iron in the eighteenth century led to the increasing use of coal, as charcoal could not be produced in sufficient quantities to meet the ever increasing requirements of smelting and was unsuitable for extracting the metal from some ores.

The development of the coal mines in the vicinity of Glasgow led to the discovery in some of the mines of important quantities of iron ore, of a kind called 'blackband ironstone'. At first this material was regarded as waste, as the methods of smelting then in use would not release the iron from the ore, but David Mushet (1772–1847) realised its value and found a way of smelting it with the aid of Nielsons's invention, the heated-air blast-furnace. This led to the prominence in the iron trade of the Glasgow ironmasters and the development of other ironstone mines. The industry expanded so quickly that by 1859 a third of all the iron produced in the United Kingdom was produced in Scotland. The development of railways and of iron-hulled ships and steam-ships at this time further increased the demand for iron and the growing wealth of the ironmasters encouraged them to go into ship construction and railway locomotive building instead of merely exporting their iron. For this the Clyde provided an ideal location, both for shipyards and for port development, allowing for the shipment of heavy engineering goods such as machinery and locomotives. But before these improvements could take place on the river a tremendous natural obstacle had to be overcome. One which made some of the cleverest engineers of the time despair of success.

Steamboat Wharf, Glasgow, in 1852

Only twelve years before this photograph was taken, in 1840, Thomas Smeaton, the great lighthouse and harbour engineer, in his survey of the Clyde, found that at Point House Ford, just east of the confluence of the Kelvin River, the depth of water of the Clyde was only fifteen inches (approximately 38cm) at low-water and at high-water a mere thirty-nine inches (100cm)! Experienced though he was, he concluded that the only solution that would allow Glasgow a deep-sea port would be to build a dam across the river and lock ships through. Fortunately the Clyde Navigational Trust, that body which has done such great work over the years, did not take his advice, but adopted the policy of building 'training' walls and by this and by land reclamation, so increased the scour of the tidal currents that, with the help of dredging, in the course of some years, the river was made deep enough to become one of the great ocean-going ports of the world. One which could be used by the largest vessels afloat. At first, as this photograph shows, the majority of vessels using the port were sailing ships. But the Clyde has played a pre-eminent part in the history of steam navigation, for the steamer itself had its birth in this region. Symington's *Charlotte Dundas* was built as a steam-tug for service on the Forth and Clyde Canal in 1801 and, on the Clyde itself, Bell opened his steam-ship service between Glasgow, Greenock and Helensburgh with his famous *Comet* in 1812. Only two years later the first steam-ship to be exported from the Clyde, the *Marjory,* was brought through the Forth and Clyde Canal to the Firth of Forth and steamed from there to the Thames. From 1840, Napier's shipyard built the first Cunard steamers and soon the annual tonnage of steam-ships being built began to exceed that of sailing vessels. The era of the iron, and later, the steel steamer had arrived and with it the great days of the Clyde as shipyard after shipyard opened on the river in the vicinity of Glasgow to take advantage of the ready availability of the three primary requirements, coal, iron and deep, sheltered water, making Glasgow Scotland's major port, in the place of Aberdeen, which had risen to fame as the port of the fast-sailing tea clippers. With this growth came the growth of ancillary industries such as the smelting of non-ferrous metals and the manufacture of brass fittings, furniture, textiles, carpets and all the many supplies and products needed for the completion and fitting out of vessels of all kinds received a tremendous stimulus. The economy of the Glasgow region had been transformed and not merely that of Glasgow but the economy of Scotland itself.

A group of ships' Engineer Officers, Glasgow, C. 1910

IN 1763, GLASGOW UNIVERSITY ENGAGED A YOUNG INSTRUMENT maker in the city to repair a model of Newcomen's 'atmospheric' single-acting steam-engine. In the course of his repairs, James Watt came to realise what an inefficient form of heat-engine the Newcomen machine was and how much needless energy loss was a part of its design. From this experience sprang the experiments, designs and patents by which Watt revolutionised the steam-engine as a source of motive power. Without his work in evolving the hot-cylinder, double-acting, compound-engine, the steam-engine as a prime-mover for ships might not have come into use as soon as it did.

The *Charlotte Dundass* and the *Comet* opened the way, both engined by machinery of a type conforming to Watt's designs. With the rapid growth of the shipbuilding industry on the Clyde, it was hardly surprising that Glasgow became a centre for the training of marine engineers in which Glasgow University played a leading part. Ocean-going shipping was approaching the peak of its performance before air-transportation had begun to erode its importance in certain areas of communications. Before long, Scottish-trained Engineer Officers were to be found not only aboard steam-ships in the British Royal and Merchant Navies but aboard many vessels of other countries as well, making the high reputation of the Scottish marine engineer a matter of world-wide recognition. Here a group of these dedicated professionals, young and old, are seen in the vicinity of Glasgow in about the year 1910.

A sea life, or a life among the heather for that matter, call for a diet rich in calories, which may help to account for that compact, portable and delicious confectionery, traditional Scottish shortbread.

Shortbread

450g butter
450g sifted white flour
225g caster sugar
225g rice flour
A good pinch of salt

Cream the butter and sugar together thoroughly in a warm bowl, then mix the flours and the salt well together and sift gradually into the creamed butter and sugar, while stirring gently to ensure even incorporation. Avoid kneading or rolling and if you are lucky enough to have carved wooden shortbread moulds gently press the paste into these, otherwise form into two round cakes about 2cm in thickness. With a finger-tip make a series of indentations around the edges and place on a baking sheet covered in baking-paper. Pre-heat the oven to 190°C. (375°F.) Gas Mark 5 and bake at this setting for 20 minutes, then reduce the setting to 180°C. (350°C.) Gas Mark 4 for around a further 40 minutes, inspecting towards the end and continuing until the shortbread has acquired an even, light fawn colour. Remove from the oven and leave to cool in the mould or on the baking sheet before placing in a rack. Store in an airtight cake tin.

A busy afternoon scene of mixed traffic and pedestrians, Victoria Bridge, Glasgow, 1914

Whether arriving by land or by sea, our travellers would have come to a city as lively and bustling as it is today, but with road traffic of a very different kind. Even as late as 1914, there were comparatively few motor vehicles in evidence, the main wheeled traffic being horse-drawn carts, drays, vans, a few steam-lorries and, of course, the ubiquitous and excellent electric trams. A city's condition, flourishing or otherwise, is readily reflected in the operation and performance of its transport system, as well as in the appearance of the people who are seen in its streets. The rapid growth of industries of all kinds which had taken place since the end of the eighteenth century, extending beyond shipbuilding into alkali production and other chemical industries, dyeing, cotton and linen spinning and finishing and the manufacture of jute products as well as a considerable growth in book production and publishing, had made Glasgow, in point of size, Scotland's chief centre of urban life. In 1893, with a show of great entrepreneurial initiative, Glasgow Corporation had taken over the generation of electricity from private suppliers and, in the following year, when another private concession expired, the network of horse-drawn trams.

There was no way that the slow horse-trams could have coped with the pressure of demand for efficient communications to serve this vital urban complex and, acting quickly, Glasgow Corporation, resourcefully applied new technology to replace the horse trams with a much extended network of electric trams which was of great importance in providing the efficient public transport facilities that such a rapidly growing industrial city required. The other industry for which Glasgow may be justly proud is that of confectionery, sweets and jam making. Due to the Glasgow merchants developing trade with the West Indies, a sugar refinery had been established nearby in the eighteenth century and this and the development of flour milling led to the growth of the baking and confectionery concerns, many of which are still world renowned today. All this promoted a very rapid population expansion. In 1801, Glasgow had a population of 77,385, but by the 1860s this had increased to over 395,500. The ultra rapid industrial development of the Glasgow region had not been accompanied by an equal care for the housing of its working population. Indeed the cities of Scotland at this time were seriously behind the other rapidly growing towns in England where housing conditions were concerned. In the nineteenth century, Glasgow and Edinburgh had some of the worst slums to be found anywhere in Europe or America. The dreadful tall tenement buildings and 'wynds' made Glasgow into a kind of cold-water Naples. To see the beginning of the story of Glasgow's efforts to clean up, revitalise conditions and tackle its appalling housing problem we have to go back to 1866.

Horse Omnibuses in Argyle Street near Anderston Cross, Glasgow, 1863

THE EARLIEST FORMS OF MASS LAND TRANSPORT TO APPEAR IN Glasgow were the privately owned horse omnibuses, two of which are seen in this photograph. But the horse omnibus drawn by two horses, a vehicle whose four wheels were shod first with wrought iron and later steel tyres, could only make very slow progress over the roughly paved streets and roads of the time, which often had a surface consisting of stone setts, and the employment of more horses per vehicle was uneconomical in relation to the fares that could be collected.

A very narrow and, seemingly, unrailed ladder or stair gives access to the unrailed seating accommodation on the open roof. Even in the best of weather a journey on the top of one of these vehicles must have been an adventurous experience when the swaying and jolting of the omnibus over the rough streets is taken into account. In the winter in wind and rain one would undoubtedly have been better off walking than sitting exposed as the omnibus trundled slowly through the streets at a little above a walking pace. In such conditions there can rarely have been many places vacant inside. The stone setts comprising the street surfaces gave a most uncomfortable, vibratory ride as the iron-rimmed wooden wheels passed over them, only very slightly damped by the primitive spring suspension and particularly noisy for the inside passengers. Such inefficient vehicles could never have met the demand of the rapidly increasing numbers of Glasgwegians for effective city transport that would get them, cheaply, to and from work.

To serve a city of now around 400,000 people, some means of reducing the frictional losses became essential. Tramways were to be the answer and the experience gained of these in a number of American cities led to the setting up and development of a network of privately owned horse-drawn tramways.

Housing conditions in the city had now reached a degree of overcrowding and insanitariness that threatened and sometimes promoted the wholesale spread of epidemic diseases. In 1866 a private Bill was passed which established a housing trust enabling Glasgow Corporation to begin the Herculean task of acquiring slum properties, demolishing them and erecting improved housing for working-class people. In doing this Glasgow Corporation was in the forefront of progress, for only two other such Acts had previously appeared on the Westminster statute books and these applied to England only. So much had to be done in this gigantic undertaking, carried out against the background of a continuously rising population, that it was not until many years after the Second World War that anything like a reasonable degree of control of the housing problem could even be said to have been approached and indeed it is still a considerable one today.

Lodging houses, Glasgow, C. 1865

As in all cities where very rapid industrial growth was taking place in the nineteenth century, the incoming flood of manual workers overwhelmed the available accommodation. Because no effective legislation was in place nor any effective schemes for new building, slum landlords quickly and ruthlessly took advantage of the social pressures to crowd greater and greater numbers into the buildings which they owned, some of which were already in a semi-ruinous state. The conditions were quite as bad as those described in London by Christopher Mayhew and Dickens a little earlier. Many of the buildings had low ceilings, a great many small rooms had no windows and all had completely inadequate sanitary facilities, for no large-scale plan for a healthy sewerage system could exist without an adequate supply of clean water for the rapidly expanding population. This was an undertaking which Glasgow Corporation was already beginning to remedy, for work had started on the Loch Katrine reservoir scheme in 1851, a project that, together with their housing trust and other important public works would transform the life of the city though it would be many years before the full benefits would be realised.

It would hardly be a exaggeration to say that in 1865, conditions in large areas of Glasgow were worse than in a mediaeval town. A devastating epidemic of disease was in prospect and it was not until the early years of the twentieth century that the danger of epidemics was eliminated and the beginnings of proper urban hygiene were put in place.

The disparity of the three lodging houses seen in the photograph is interesting. McIlvenny's establishment looks grim indeed and that on its right not much better. The best of them is undoubtedly the temperance establishment on the right, where a building with decently high ceilings has been acquired. Above its entrance swings a sign of a crown containing a teapot, which reminds us of the tremendous social problem of alcoholism in a rapidly changing environment.

The shop under the arcade appears to sell requisites for the dairy such as tun-dishes, butter-working tubs and a dash-churn, while the shop on the extreme left is an artists' colourman.

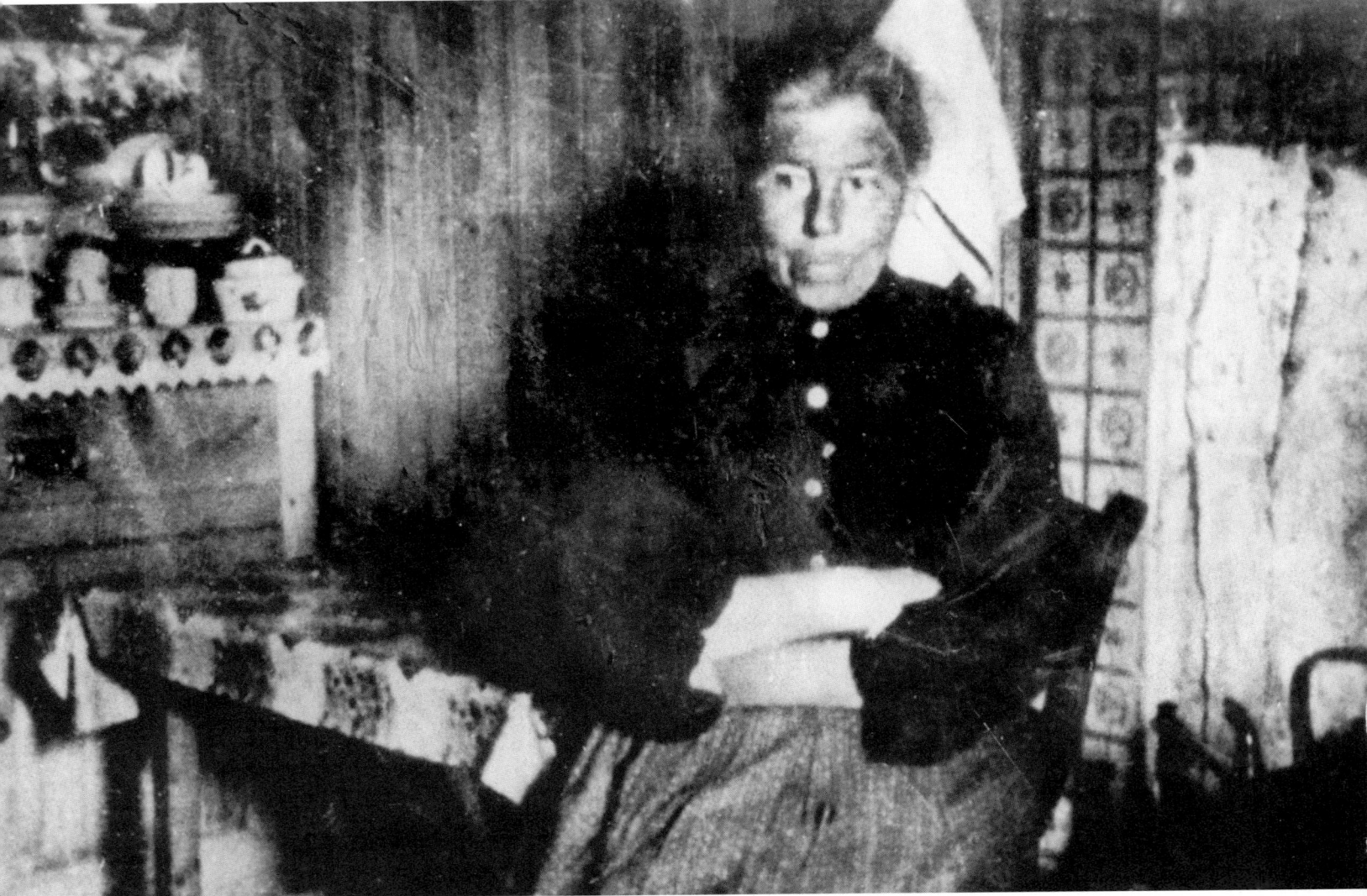

An old woman in the Gorbals, Glasgow, C. 1890

IN SCOTLAND, IN THE YEAR 1861, ALMOST 26,000 HOUSES HAD NO window. A great many of the poorer people in the cities lived in high tenement buildings where many rooms were ventilated only through the chimney flue and some had no fireplace. By 1900, the number of windowless houses had been reduced to around 200. Other aspects of sanitation were equally disastrous in the 1860s. A beginning had been made by the enterprising Glasgow Corporation in 1859 by making Loch Katrine into a reservoir for supplying the city. This not only made clean drinking water available on a mass scale but enabled a main-drainage sewerage system to be put in hand. The Glasgow Corporation Housing Trust, established in 1861, commenced to tackle the unhealthy slum housing by buying out slum landlords and constructing new accommodation which had proper sanitation built in, but even thirty years later there were considerable areas of the city where conditions were still deplorable, as this little pokey room shows. Note the deep cracks in the wall of the fireplace. In such conditions enteritis and tuberculosis were very prevalent and, as late as 1900, there was an outbreak of plague, the last in the United Kingdom, always a risk in a great port where housing conditions could lead to a prevalence of rats and fleas. It is touching to see the attempts that have been made to brighten up the little room, with trimmed printed oil-cloth arranged on the shelves of the little dresser and an oil-cloth on the tiny table. Oil-cloth (American Cloth) had only been introduced from the US a few years previously and provided the first form of cheap artificial surface that could be easily cleaned with a damp cloth, before the arrival of our modern synthetic surfaces. It was a great boon to poor people at the time. A clean dish-cloth hangs beside the fireplace and, on the dresser are a pathetic little collection of cups, saucers and dishes. A black kettle provides the only means of supplying hot water. The photograph has been taken by the use of flash-powder and shows that the natural illumination level in the room must have been very low. Where economic growth or decline is taking place rapidly, the population at large is always subjected to extreme stresses unless a careful watch on social conditions is maintained and effective measures are taken in time by a competent authority with the power and the finances to act appropriately.

John Rae's Public House, Castle Street, Glasgow, C. 1900

Glasgow is famous for its public houses today and was so when this photograph was taken. There has always been a strong tradition of serving food in the Glasgow pubs and it is tantalising that at this famous one in Castle Street, it is just not possible to make out the intriguing Bill of Fare, chalked up on the slate before the entrance, except, that is, for the first three items on the menu, 'Beef Soup', 'Mutton Broth' and 'Roast Beef'. The establishment is a clean and comfortable looking one and has installed a startling innovation, incandescent electric light, which makes this photograph interesting in another way, for in it we see indications of the three stages of artificial lighting that came to the city. Just beside the waiter is one of the remaining public street lighting standards of the oil-lamp era, a most elegant cast-iron lamp-standard from the time prior to the introduction of gas street-lighting. We must not forget that, while oil-lamp street lighting was introduced by the Arabs, Cordoba being the first city in the world to be so lit, coal-gas lighting itself was invented by a Scot, William Murdoch, who used it domestically, in Redruth for several years before installing a gas-lighting plant in a factory in Manchester. The next important development was the improvement in Murdoch's inefficient burners, by another famous Scottish engineer, the Glasgow inventor of the hot-air blast-furnace, J B Neilson, who invented the 'fish tail' burner, the first that could be fitted into a glass globe, in 1820.

Glasgow Corporation took over the production of gas from private hands in 1869 and extended its supply widely throughout the city. We are reminded of all this by the two large ornate gas lanterns on either side of John Rae's doorway. The final stage, in which the Corporation became the supplier of electric power, began in 1893 and this is recalled by the incandescent lamps in the windows, though these, judging by their design, can hardly be earlier than the early years of the twentieth century. Then, as now, Glasgow contained many Irish people and we are reminded of this by the notice on the right hand side of the entrance; 'Scottish and Irish Whiskies. Well Matured.' The advertising of both kinds of spirit shows us that the existence of pubs many of whose patrons are Irish has been a feature of Glasgow for over a century and is likely to continue for many years to come. The mixture of things Scottish and Irish has for long characterised the atmosphere of the city and given it a unique cultural ambience hardly to be found elsewhere in Scotland and is surely one of the factors which give Glasgow its variety and liveliness. Long may it so continue.

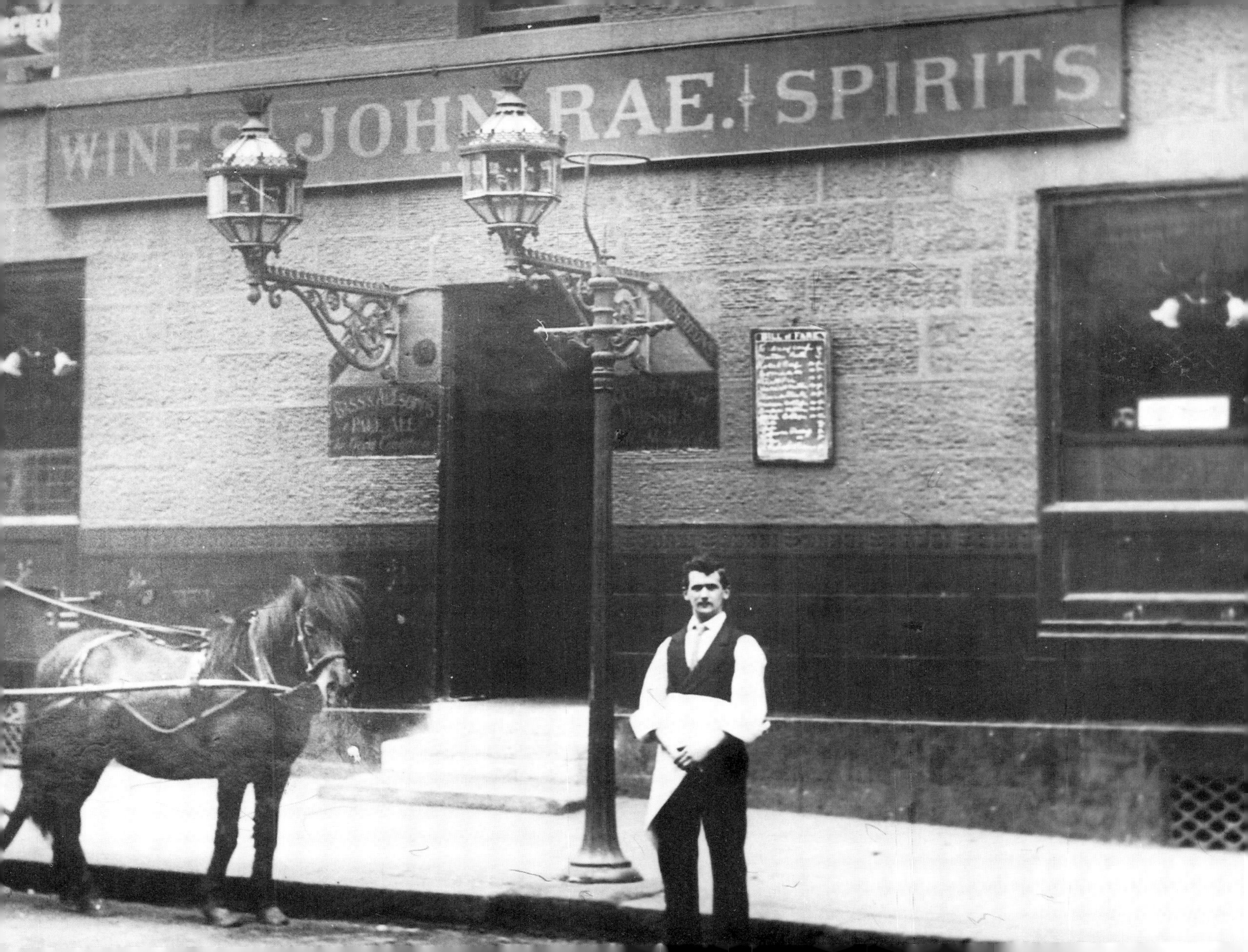
WINES JOHN RAE. SPIRITS

Springburn Post Office, Glasgow, 1900

Electricity brought with it another innovation besides flexible lighting techniques. It introduced the era of telecommunications through the electric telegraph and the telephone, the nineteenth-century equivalents of our present world-wide network of digital satellite communications.

From halfway through the nineteenth century, electric telegraphy had become fairly widely available and the Atlantic Ocean had first been spanned by cable in 1857, a development made possible by Lord Kelvin's researches into the difficulties of transmitting messages through long distance cables, while, by the year of his death in 1907, such cables had become world wide. The telegraph boy, seen standing outside the post-office was an essential, terminal link in this international telecommunications network, which, in the UK was run by the Post Office. He provided the final delivery to the addressee, carrying the telegram in the small leather pouch attached to his belt and receiving a modest tip when this service was rendered. Those who wished to send telegrams had either to send completed forms by their servants to the local telegraph-office, or go there themselves to fill them in; but it had the advantage over the fax systems of the present, that no users had to install any expensive apparatus and deliveries could be made anywhere. It also gave employment in a widespread way that fax systems do not and was surprisingly efficient, so much so that it was still in use up to the 1960s in Paris, in spite of the available telephone service, the 'petit bleu' being used on all kind of social occasions as well as for business. Fax has only succeeded in fully replacing it for the latter purpose.

The telephone was emerging as a fairly widespread public service and it was to be more than a quarter of a century before visual matter could be widely transmitted over wires and, even then, very imperfectly. So effectively were these public services run that there was a minimal competition from private couriers who had largely gone out of general business after the introduction of the 'penny post'.

Another important activity of the Glasgow area is shown by the advertisement for Bells' Dye Works, Paisley. Dyeing had been an important industry for well over a century and a quarter and David Dale had invented his 'Turkey Red' dye for carpets. The textile industries' demand for bleaches and dyes led to a rapid advance of the chemical industry at St Rollox.

The two apprentice surgical limb makers remind us that the expression 'prosthesis' had not come into the general vocabulary as it has today. Then there were so few artificial components of the human body that they were enumerated individually. Today they are so numerous that a special generic term is necessary.

SPRINGBURN POST OFFICE

Trongate, Glasgow, 1914

Looking down Glasgow's Trongate, from the corner of Stockwell Street, the most prominent architectural feature is the Tron Steeple, emerging from the top of a square tower under which the southern pavement runs beneath arches. It represents the surviving remains of St Mary's Church, founded in 1637.

The name Trongate comes from that municipal device of the sixteenth and seventeenth centuries, situated near the city gate, the 'tron' or public weighing-beam, against which merchants, weights were checked to insure that their dealings with the public were honest (page 119).

In the middle of the eighteenth century, Sir Francis Dashwood established a club of young Georgian 'bloods' and figures such as Bubb Doddington and John Wilkes at his house at Medmenham on the Thames, not far from Maidenhead, where François Rabelais' slogan of the Abbey of Theleme *Fay ce que voudras*, was carved above a doorway. This group of roisterers and gamblers became known as The Franciscans or The Monks of Medmenham and, later, their club was named The Hell-Fire Club. It flourished as a reaction to the polite civilities of the Age of Reason and soon had established itself in premises in London. Later similar clubs were founded in Dublin and other cities, including Glasgow.

Lurid tales of Satanism came to adorn these institutions and form around them a mythical miasma which disguised the fact that nothing more than very commonplace debauchery seems to have been involved. However, in 1793, some of the members of the Glasgow club got badly out of hand and set fire to St Mary's, Trongate, which was destroyed but for the tower and spire, so that its remains today commemorate the blackest outrage committed by any of the rake-hell clubs of the eighteenth century which had evolved from The Franciscans.

At half past three on a summer afternoon of 1914, this busy street is crowded with shoppers and there is no indication of the event which, only a few weeks later, was to transform the nation and usher in a new age where nothing would ever be the same again. To us, this summer sunshine that bathes normal, everyday activity in the Trongate is not without a sense of tragedy when one thinks of the carnage to come, the waste of millions of lives and the waste of incalculable millions of public resources that could have so greatly assisted the Glasgow Corporation in its Herculean task. The stagnation and economic depression that followed further hampered balanced civic development as did the great Wall Street collapse in the 1930s.

CECIL
RESTAURANT
R. FRENCH
JEWELLER
HOTEL
RESTAURANT
WINES
Swansons

MARYHILL
St VINCENT Pl
863
GALLOWGATE-JAMAICA ST-PAISLEY RD

Glasgow Trams, 1914

GLASGOW IS NOT MERELY THE LARGEST COMMERCIAL CENTRE IN Scotland, it is the seat of an ancient university, founded in 1450. In 1846, a young man, born in Belfast, Northern Ireland, and the son of the professor of mathematics at Glasgow university, was appointed, at the astonishingly early age of twenty-two, to the chair of natural philosophy there. William Thomson, later Lord Kelvin of Largs, was to become one of the greatest physicists of the nineteenth century and to promote the advancement of that science to a greater degree than any other until the time of Einstein, Bohr and Rutherford. There was hardly a field of technology that he did not transform by his lively and creative mind and his indefatigable researches, while remaining, to the end of his days, a modest and approachable personality, excelling in encouraging young people to develop their talents.

It is hardly surprising, that having a man of such distinction in their midst, the public administrators of the city showed so much initiative in technological developments, particularly in the use of electricity, a field to which Lord Kelvin had devoted a major portion of his attention.

Trams were an interesting form of transport, the conductor was the captain, not the driver, and in a tramway system based on overhead supply, as in Glasgow, he could, in emergency, disconnect the supply simply by pulling on the trolley rope.

As the photograph shows, the Corporation's electric lighting had taken over from their gas lighting, so far as the main thoroughfares were concerned, using carbon-arc lamps. These remained the chief type of lamp used in the main streets until the introduction of the mercury-vapour lamp in the 1930s.

The Corporation had shown great initiative in electricity generation and its efficient application to urban transportation. Had this same initiative been shown by the proprietors of the privately owned railways, following upon the experiments of Robert Davidson (page 110), the electrification of at least some of the railways in Scotland might have been brought about long before their electrification in England. But the whole balance of development in Glasgow was to be upset by the disaster of a World War, when the shipping industry would find itself forced to develop in a way that would leave it vulnerable when the great conflict was over. Meanwhile, in this war, the urban transport system based on electric trams could continue on its home-produced power supply, whereas buses would have needed the continual importation of fuel from overseas. St Enoch's Station used to serve the South Western Railway and was the station at which the English Midland Railway passengers arrived in Glasgow.

Paddle Steamers at the Broomielaw, Glasgow, C. 1900

GLASGOW IS NOT MERELY A CITY AND A PORT. LIKE VENICE, IT IS the centre of an archipelago and a city where water transport forms an important part of everyday life. The hub of this aspect of the town's life is the partly covered quay known as the Broomielaw. Most of the ferries connecting with the communities along the Clyde itself, the adjacent sea-lochs and the nearer off-shore islands arrive and depart here today, as they did at the turn of the century. The paddle steamers remind us that it was the Scots who first applied steam-power to water-transport, beginning with the *Charlotte Dundass* on the Clyde - Forth canal and later, on the river itself, with the famous *Comet*. For almost two centuries the Broomielaw has been the point of departure for steam ferries and a few still call there even today. No one who is on their first visit to Scotland should miss the experience of travelling on a ferry paddle-steamer and seeing its engines in action. A compound marine engine on a screw steamer inspired Oscar Wilde to write the lines:

> *The muffled steersman at the wheel*
> *Is but a shadow in the gloom,*
> *While in the throbbing engine-room*
> *Leap the long rods of polished steel.*

Though the action of a paddle-steamer's engines, with their oscillating cylinders, is different, it is still an unforgettable experience of rhythmical musical motions which no turbine or motor-ship can provide and should on no account be missed by anyone with an interest in the sculptural or the musical.

The members of a community who daily migrate by ferry develop quite a different mentality from those who journey by commuter train. The open perspectives on a great estuary and the exposure to the weather give a stimulation to travellers that the underground train can never supply, convenient though it may be, so the life of a considerable part of the city's inhabitants is moulded, yet again, by the great river. Another link in the chain that makes Glasgow unique is forged.

Glasgow people are sociable and conversational and ferries lend themselves to this exchange more effectively than any other form of transport. Into the Broomielaw came all the news from the islands and all the life of a brimming river and it was and is also the gateway to freedom.

Once aboard ship and out into the stream, the city is quickly left behind, in a very little time one has enchanting vistas of water and hills, has felt the muted surges of the ocean and gained deserted Atlantic solitudes on the shores of lovely islands. From no city is the act of departure made so easy and pleasant.

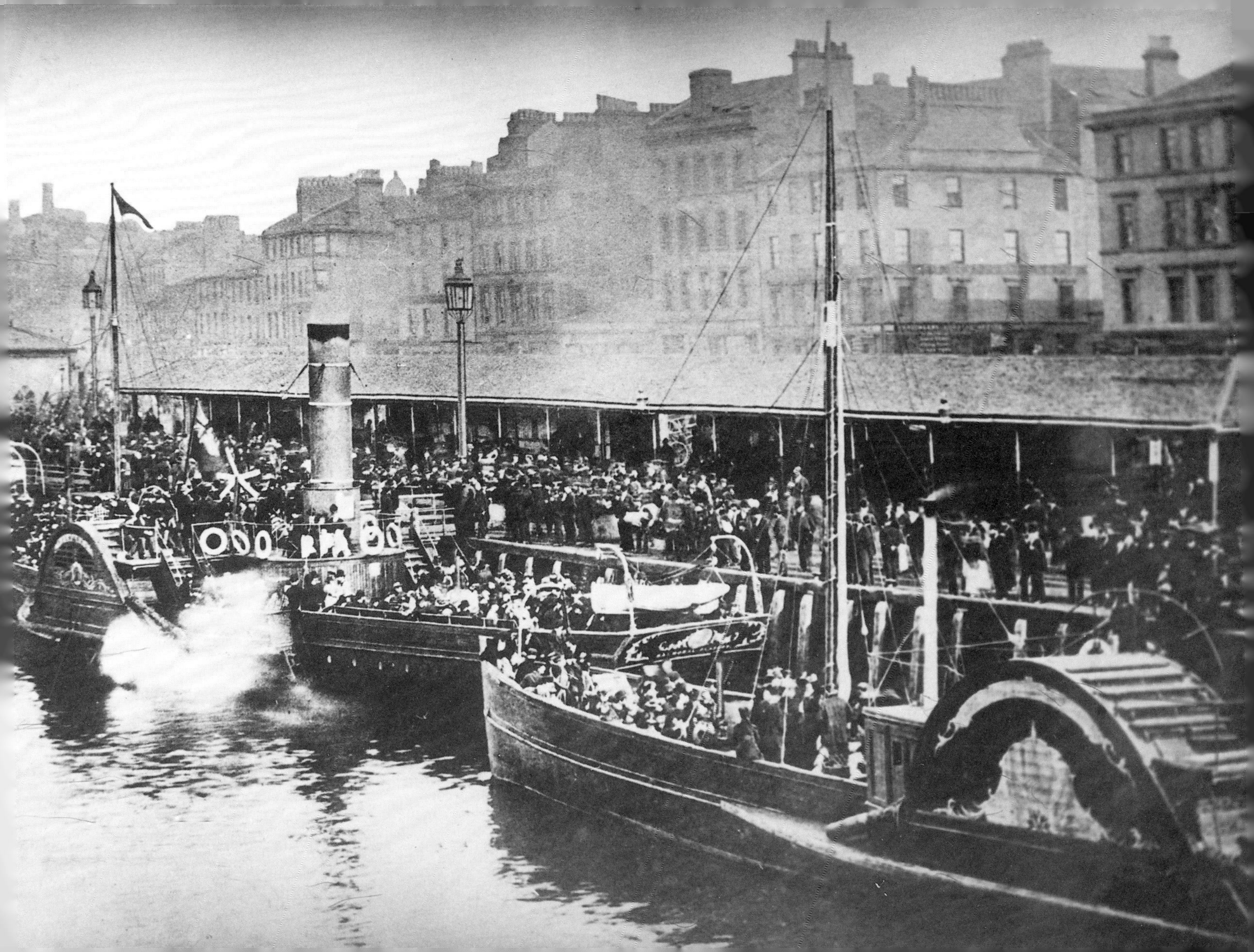

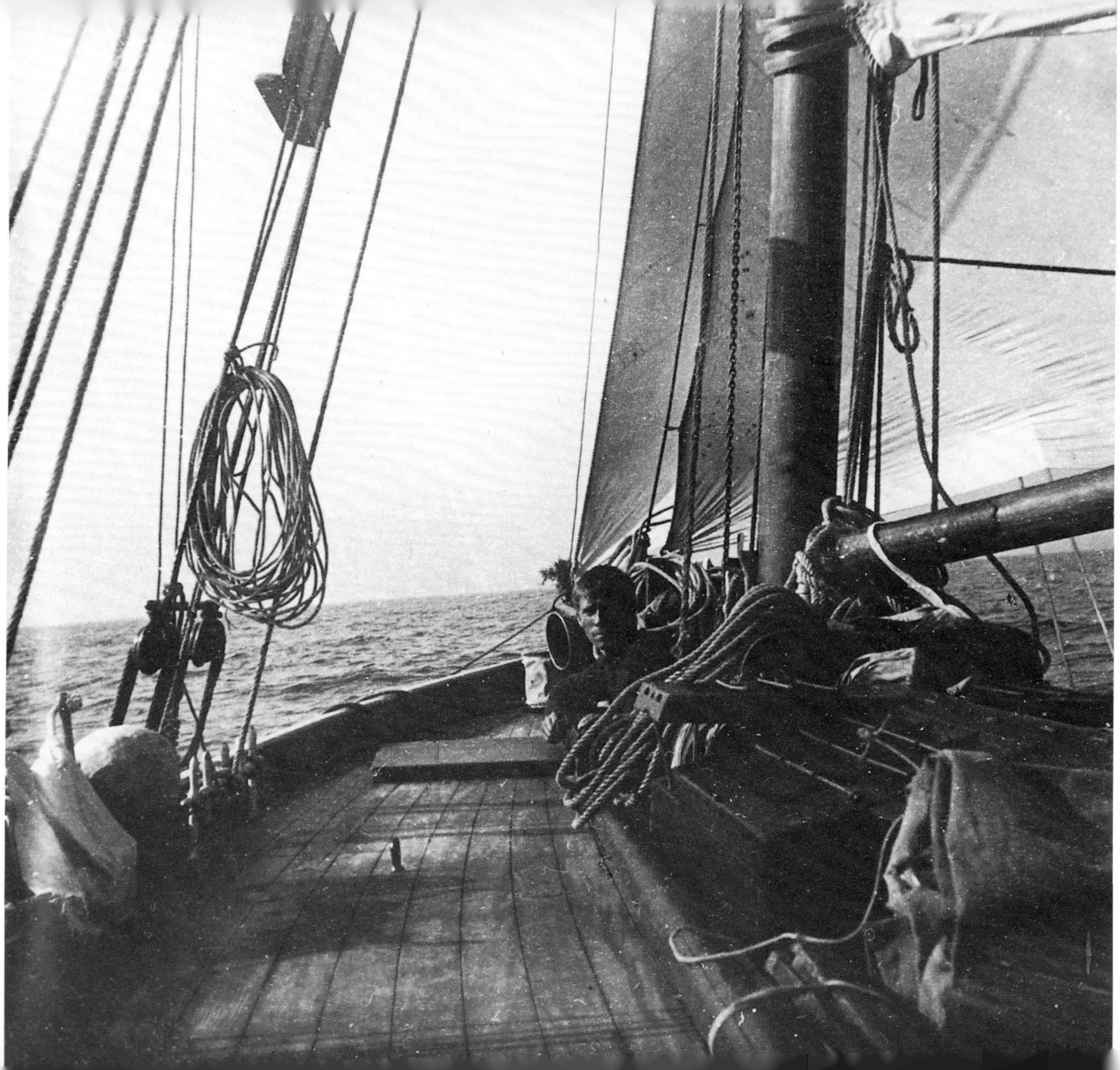

Heading for the Isles, 1895

Few large cities in these islands have in their vicinity waters so attractive to the yachtsman as Glasgow. No greater change of atmosphere from that of urban life can be found than in putting to sea in a five or ten-tonner and leaving miles of living water between one's daily occupation and one's present recreation. The delicious sensation that recall is no easy matter is, in itself, a tonic. Or perhaps one should say was, for the arrival of that excellent safety device radio and what can only be described as that impertinently intrusive device the cell-net telephone require strong-mindedness before the freedom of the 1890s can be regained and enjoyed. A great variety of safe anchorages abound and what a selection of diversified islands are within easy reach, from the barest to the most lush. If the range of cuisine aboard a small yacht should pall, the most delicious food is available ashore from the simplest to the most sophisticated. Should the weather turn bad, there are many safe harbours, but, for cruising, experience, someone aboard with a good knowledge of local tides and currents and a set of good charts and sailing directions are all essentials.

One cannot sail these waters without a sense of adventure and what an appetite the clean air and activity gives, but as there is no room for a sea-going butler on a ten-tonner, one's preparations must be adequately made and a couple of fishing-rods on board is a good idea.

Travelling in this way at the right season gives one a rare delight, that of eating mackerel when drawn straight from the sea, for in this condition their taste is incomparable. The finest way of treating them is a long-tried, traditional Scots recipe and one quite suitable for a small boat.

Mackerel Fried in Oatmeal.

As soon as the fish are killed, behead and gut them, remove their tails, wash them inside and out with seawater and toss them in a plastic bag containing coarse pin-head oatmeal seasoned to taste with salt and freshly ground black pepper, supplying more of the same if needed. Then fry them rapidly in hot vegetable oil (the original used to be lard), drain them on a pad of kitchen paper and serve on hot plates with lemon-wedges beside them. To have a few extra lemon wedges and the black pepper mill standing by on the cabin table does no harm. On a wet day, a dram of whisky taken at the same time and one can truly say one is *bien réstauré*.

Pollock can be treated in the same way and are surprisingly good when as fresh as this, but mackerel and herring are best for this simple and delightful recipe, which, with good potatoes boiled in their skins and dried, is a dish fit for a Scottish, or indeed any other, king.

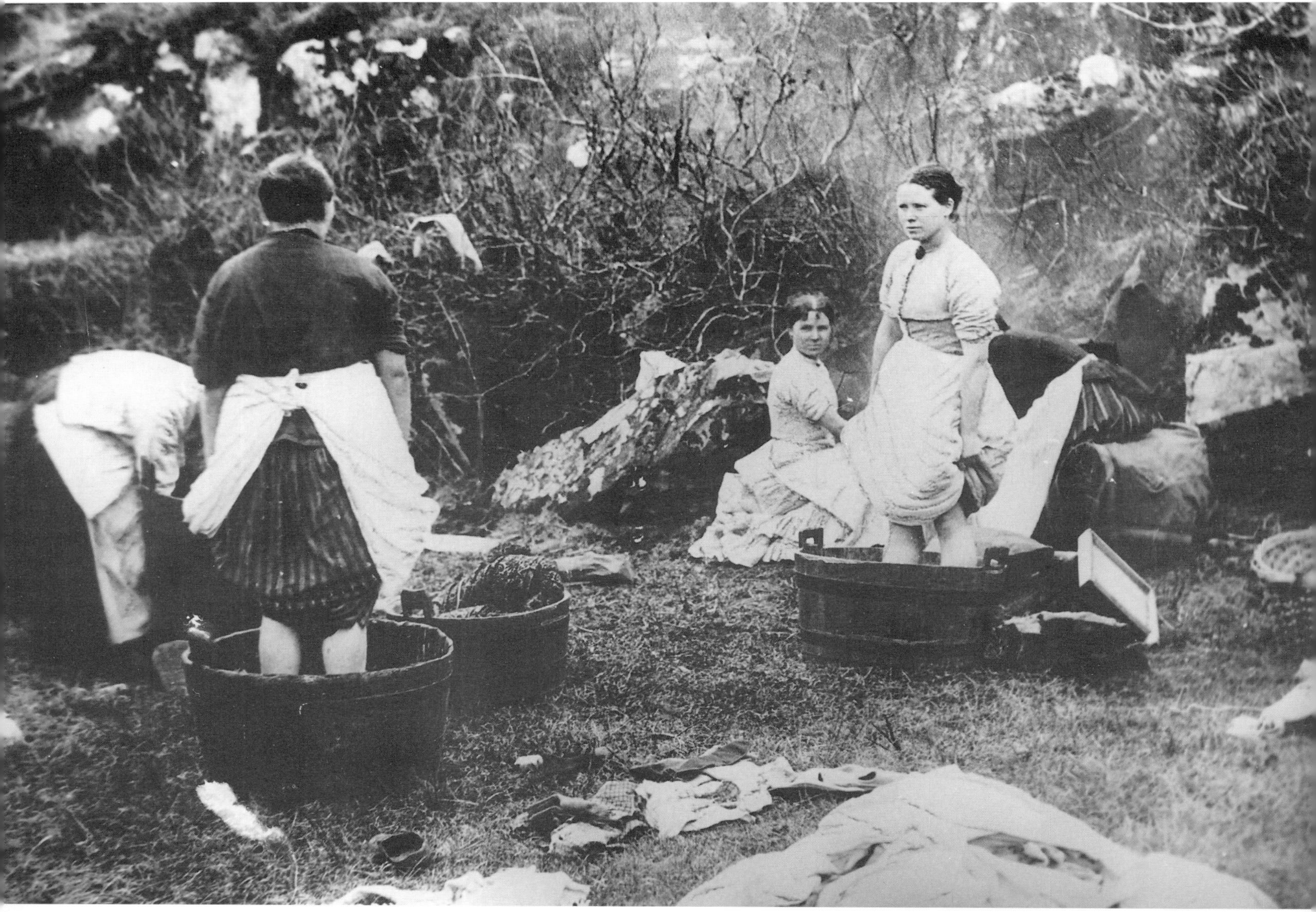

Laundry work, Isle of Skye, 1880s

IN THE LAST YEARS OF THE NINETEENTH CENTURY, A SHORT JOURNEY by sea could seem like a long journey back in time, a journey of over a hundred years into a period that had long been left behind in the cities. The laundry techniques still in use then in parts of Scotland were those such as might today be found on the banks of the Indus. At a time when the smallest display of ankle was regarded as indecorous, photographers, even distinguished ones, had a perfect obsession with the everyday work of these girls, who were often being pestered for photographs like this and their natural reaction is to be seen in the annoyance shown on their faces. One can hardly blame them.

On the islands, the transition from the old economy of cattle, sheep, fish and barley to over reliance on the treacherous potato had advanced to the state of recurrent famines, though none as severe as the great Irish disaster. In spite of the richness of the well tended sandy, machair land areas, which, though fertile, were not very extensive and the exploitation of the sea for fishing and for seaweed, for manure and for kelp-burning, pressures of a rising population had long been forcing emigration to increase and, at the time of this photograph, mass tourism had not yet begun.

Gaelic was the everyday speech and it has survived with considerable success, but we should remember that it is as important to preserve the culture of gastronomy as it is that of language; after all, gastronomy is a language of communication and a very convincing one too. On many of the western isles and the coast of Scotland generally, mussels are readily to be had and are easily made into a really delicious soup.

Mussel Brose

Around 40 fresh live mussels
600ml hot milk
600ml water
salt and freshly milled black pepper
25g lightly toasted oat-flakes

Discard any of the mussels that are open. Wash the remainder well, scrubbing them with a hard brush and put them into the cold water in a saucepan, cover the saucepan and put it onto a low heat until the mussels open, which will be in about five minutes, then strain the liquid into another saucepan through a hair-sieve or a fine chinois to remove any sand, grit or shell fragments. Shell and de-beard the mussels and reserve in a hot dish. Boil up the mussel liquor and add to it the hot milk, season to taste, then add to it a cupful of previously toasted oatflakes, stirring rapidly so that the oatflakes form 'knots', take from the heat and allow it to come just off the boil, add the mussels to re-heat them but on no account allow the soup to boil. Taste again for seasoning, adjust if necessary, and serve with hot, fresh, crusty wholemeal bread.

Wringing Blankets, Isle of Skye, 1880s

Here the atmosphere is relieved by the classical dignity of the two foreground figures and we are reminded of the difficulties involved in laundry-work before the appearance of the mangle, but notice the introduction of the two staves into the woollen mass that allow the women to get a sufficient mechanical advantage to put enough torsion into the cloth to squeeze out the water, no easy matter where heavy blankets are concerned. One of these staves, which were also used for beating the clothes, is lying on the ground to the right. At the left, the cast-iron cauldron set over a fire among the rocks and the accompanying pail of cold water show how the temperature was controlled to allow the girls to tread the clothes without scalding their feet. Just beyond the hearth there is an interesting little pile of more or less uniformly sized stones. Could these be a relic of earlier times when metal vessels were expensive and not so readily available and earthen-ware vessels of water could not be stood directly over the fire were in use – the water was heated by dropping heated stones into it?

How stony, thin and poor the soil appears in this vicinity, a film of humus over the rocky bones of the island. In such conditions wheat cannot be grown effectively, but oats and barley can grow where wheat can not and oats not only give us that wonderful savoury staple food, porridge, but that delicious delicacy of the Scottish table, oatcakes, made with oatmeal flour which, unfortunately, is not as readily to be found abroad as oat-flakes, though it is now getting easier to get the oatcakes themselves. Here is a most excellent recipe for them, most kindly given to me by Mrs Jill Black, of Clachan Corrach, Iona, whose experience and skill produce oatcakes of a wafer thinness and delicious flavour.

Mrs Black's Oatcakes

2 cups medium oatmeal flour
120ml (approximately) water
1 cup (barely) plain white flour
salt and freshly ground white pepper to taste
125g butter or margarine

Sift flours and mix well together with the salt and pepper, then rub the fat into the dry ingredients, adding gradually enough water to make a moist, soft dough. Liberally strew your pastry-board with wholemeal brown flour and roll out the oatcake dough very thinly, cut into rounds and re-work the pieces left over adding a little more water if it has become too dry. Place the rounds on a baking sheet and bake in a moderate to hot oven for 15 to 20 minutes, until the surface of the oatcakes is a light golden colour

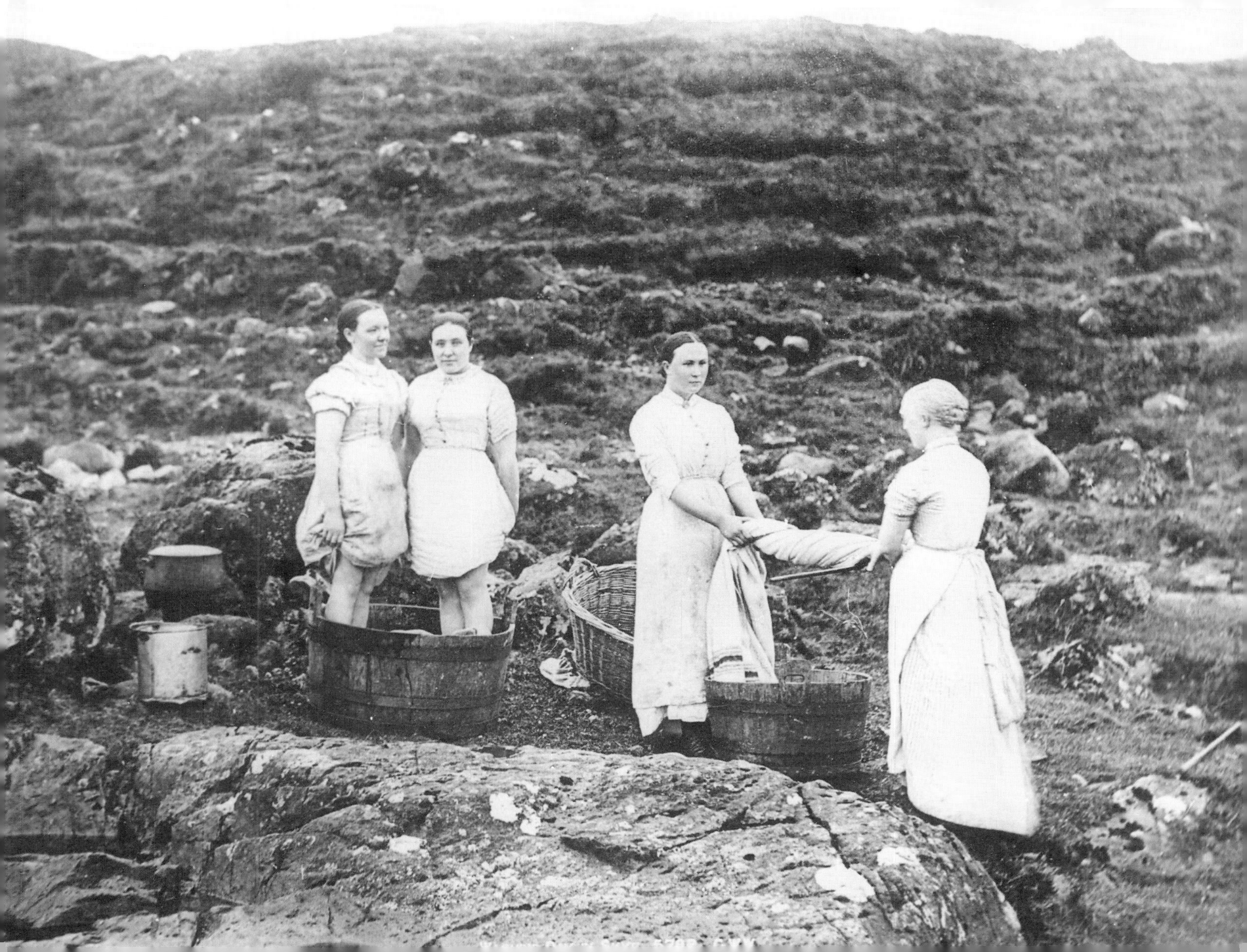

A crofter's family, 1880s

With the break up of the clan system of social responsibilities and the introduction of commercial farming and sheep raising for distant markets, the lot of the small holders in the outlying parts of Scotland declined steadily. This economic decline was accelerated by the spread of the 'famine root', the untrustworthy potato, which, because it enabled subsistence farming to be carried out on a fraction of the land needed for growing other products, led to the dividing up of the small holdings into still smaller ones with the increasing real impoverishment of those living on, as distinct from those owning, the land. The disparity between the rich and the poor grew fast until conditions such as we see in large parts of The Third World today were common in the remoter parts of Scotland and remedial measures never seemed to be able to keep up with the growth of impoverishment. The grandmother, slumped at the foot of the door, is probably no older than sixty and the faces of the young people are already marked with disillusion and despair. They are, however, all shod, which they might not be in a similar Irish photograph.

The small crofters tried to squeeze out a living by combining small-boat fishing and kelp-burning with farming, but the utmost local ingenuity could not keep going in the face of the relentless economic pressures. It was the rapid spread of these conditions that led to the establishment of the Congested Districts Board, which endeavoured, in both Scotland and Ireland, to reverse the trend by developing alternative forms of employment and assisting the fishing and other local industries. No initiatives of this kind however could prevail against the commercial development of the steam-trawler fishing fleets of the East Coast ports, made possible by the rail connections to the big markets of the South. Even Ullapool felt these pressures. Emigration from the Western Isles continued, leading to isolation and cultural impoverishment, through the departure of so many young people before the oral traditions of poetry and song could be handed on to them.

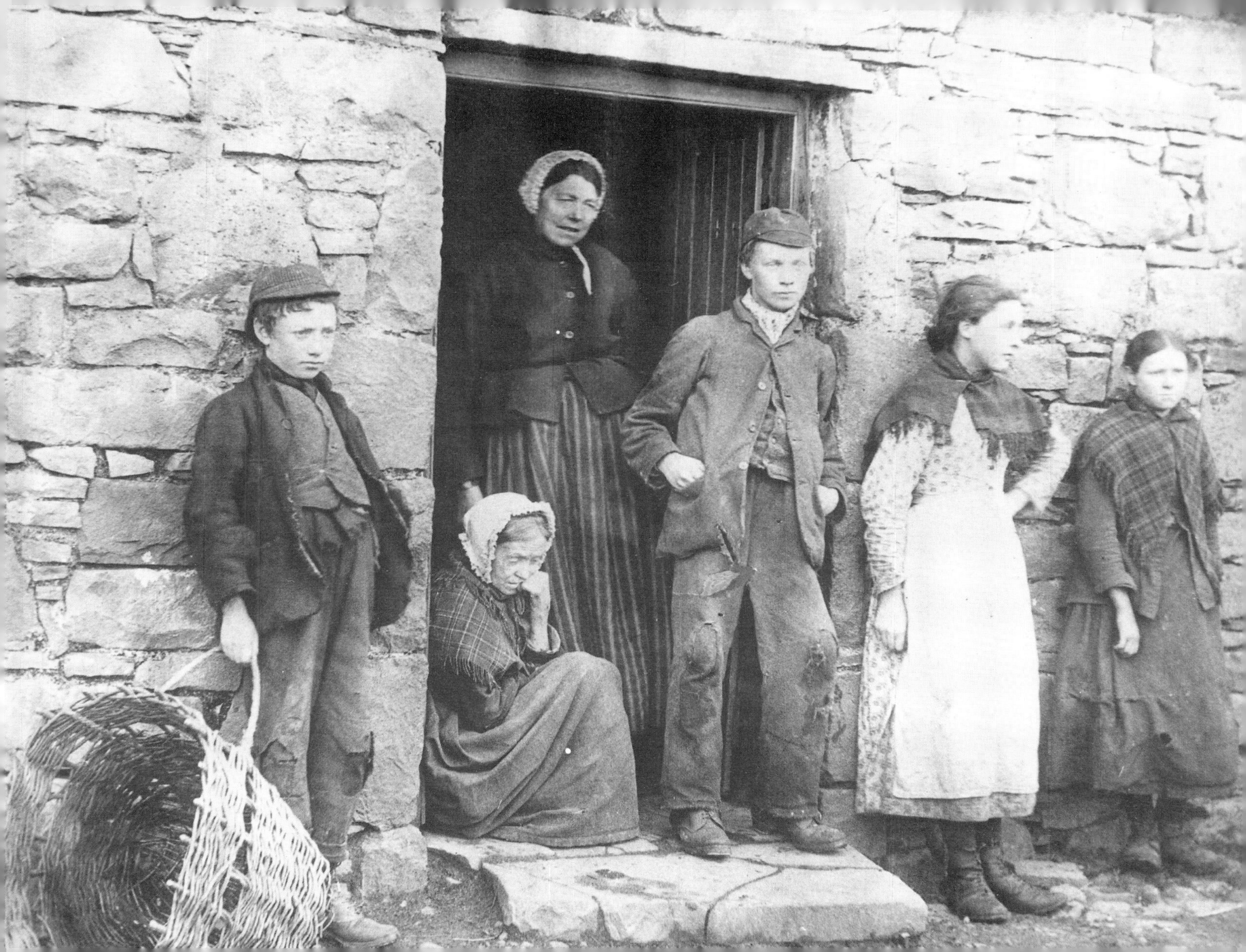

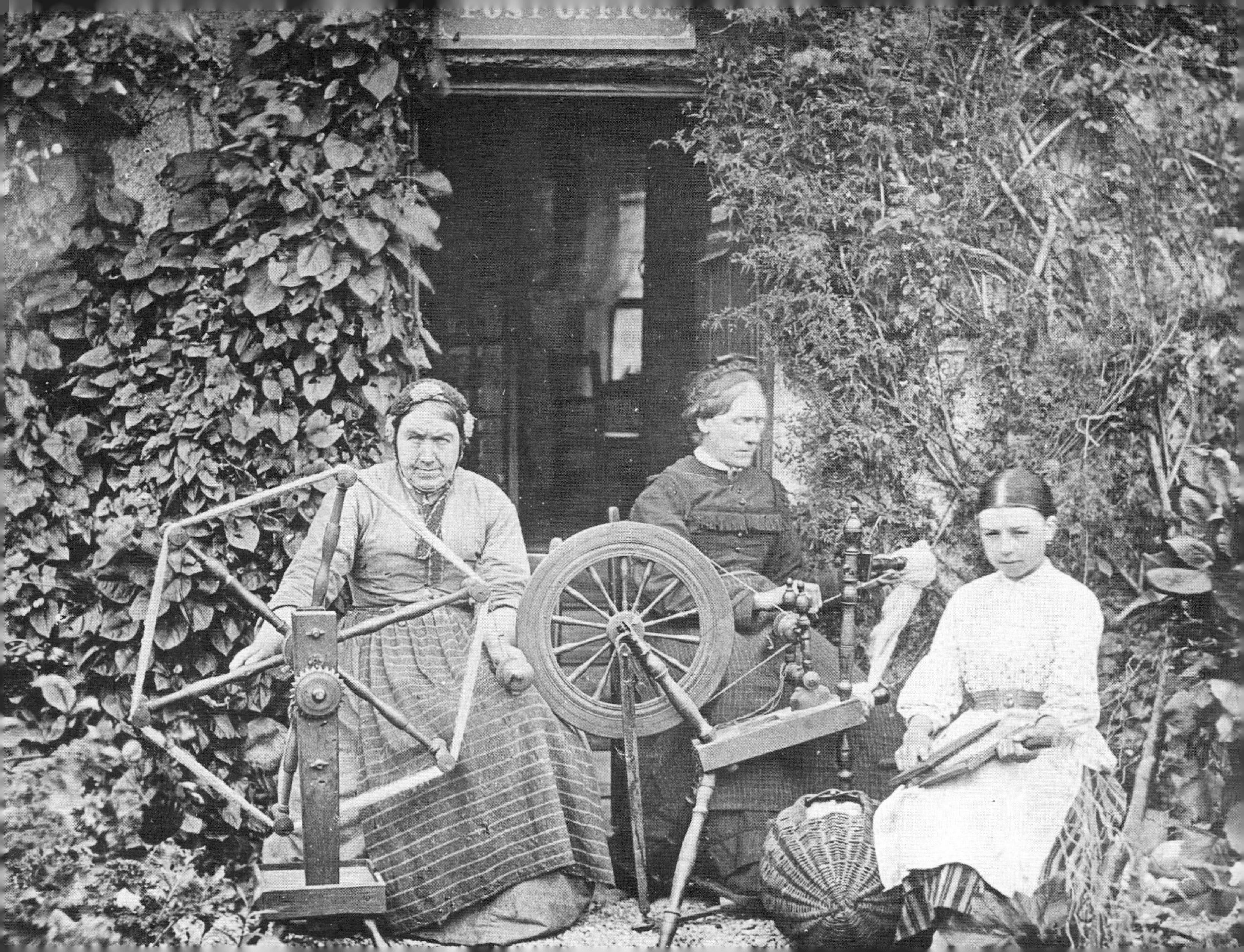
POST OFFICE

Winding, Spinning and Carding Wool, 1880s

Here is a glimpse of a more prosperous family at work, interesting because it shows the operations of carding, spinning and winding wool which were at the time, along with dyeing and weaving, important cottage industries.

Between 1780 and 1880 great changes in the breeds of sheep had taken place, reflected in corresponding differences in the quality and character of the yarns and the tweeds that were made from them,. The bleaching and dyeing techniques had changed too. Chlorine was first used for bleaching at the suggestion of James Watt in Glasgow in 1787. Charles Tennant, a Glasgow bleacher, later discovered and used the more convenient chloride of lime for the same purpose. Although the Scottish chemical industry early made available a number of dyes such as Dale's Red, the ancient dyeing techniques using natural sources such as gorse flowers, blackberry juice and heather extracts still continue to the present day in the production of fine tweeds.

After shearing, the fleeces were washed and dried and the coarser tangles removed. The teased-out wool was then put into round wicker-work containers called wool-baskets with a small opening at the top, such as the example seen by the young girl's feet. She is 'carding'. She takes a small quantity of the fleece from the wool-basket and works it backwards and forwards between the two flat paddles which have the points of closely set rows of nails protruding through their inner surfaces, the nail tips bent into a uniform curve. In this way the wool of the fleece is drawn into parallel alignment so that when passed to the spinner (at the centre of the group) she can, by the use of the spindle rotated by the treadle and her dextrous fingers, spin the wool into yarn, which is then wound loosely on the jack-winder at the left to give the loose hanks of yarn ready for bleaching or dyeing, or for weaving directly, giving a tweed full of the natural lanoline of the fleece which makes it water resistant and very comfortable to wear in a knitted fabric. The spinner is using a 'cocked-up Saxony wheel', which has the advantage over the more primitive hand-turned wheel of leaving both the spinner's hands free.

The activity seen here was usually conducted indoors and would appear to have been posed outside for the sake of the photographer, whose plates were not sufficiently fast for him to take a photograph indoors without asking his sitters to remain still for too long.

Another clue to the prosperity of this family is that they are running a local post-office. It must never be forgotten that when that great medium of social revolution the State-run 'penny post' was introduced, it not only immensely improved communications but offered a steady, continuous employment which helped to stabilise many small local communities.

A rich landlord's house on Islay. Croquet on the lawn, C.1880

With the very rapid growth of industry in the Clyde Valley and vicinity, it was hardly surprising that some large private fortunes were made, as they had earlier been made in the tobacco and sugar importing businesses, the beneficiaries often spending a portion of their wealth to acquire land and often to build modern houses such as this one on Islay, where a family are seen playing croquet on the back lawn. The wide, hooped skirts, originally introduced in this form by Worth, are still being worn and evidently require a certain amount of stand-off when using a croquet mallet, but the mystery is where are the croquet-hoops? Played without these and the stick marking the starting and finishing point, the game does not appear to be a very serious one. Probably the children are being taught how to play. The sun-dial, too, cannot be taken very seriously as it seems to be sited far too close to the house. Perhaps it is not a sundial.

Architecturally, the house has a curiously urban, one might almost say suburban air, in which convenience has dominated considerations of overall architectural form, resulting in a an impression of settled comfort rather than imposing structure.

The gardener has arranged for plenty of ventilation in the green-houses as the day would seem to be a warm one and perhaps the ladies and the children would appreciate a glass of lemonade after their croquet lesson.

Lemonade.

12 ripe lemons
225g vanilla sugar
2.75L cold water
a small sprig of mint or lemon balm

Measure the cold water into a large saucepan with a lid and add to it the sugar and mint or lemon balm and put it on a gentle heat, stirring occasionally to allow the sugar to dissolve. Halve and squeeze the lemons, adding both the juice and the empty lemon-halves to the saucepan as soon as the sugar is dissolved. Bring slowly to the boil and simmer until a fork shows the lemon peel to be tender, then take from the heat and allow to grow cold, covered, in a cool place. When cold, *passé* the lemonade through a large chinois into a capacious jug and place in the refrigerator to chill. If a sweeter lemonade is preferred, more ordinary sugar, to taste, may be added when heating. To serve, add a small fresh sprig of mint and lemon balm and a few ice-cubes.

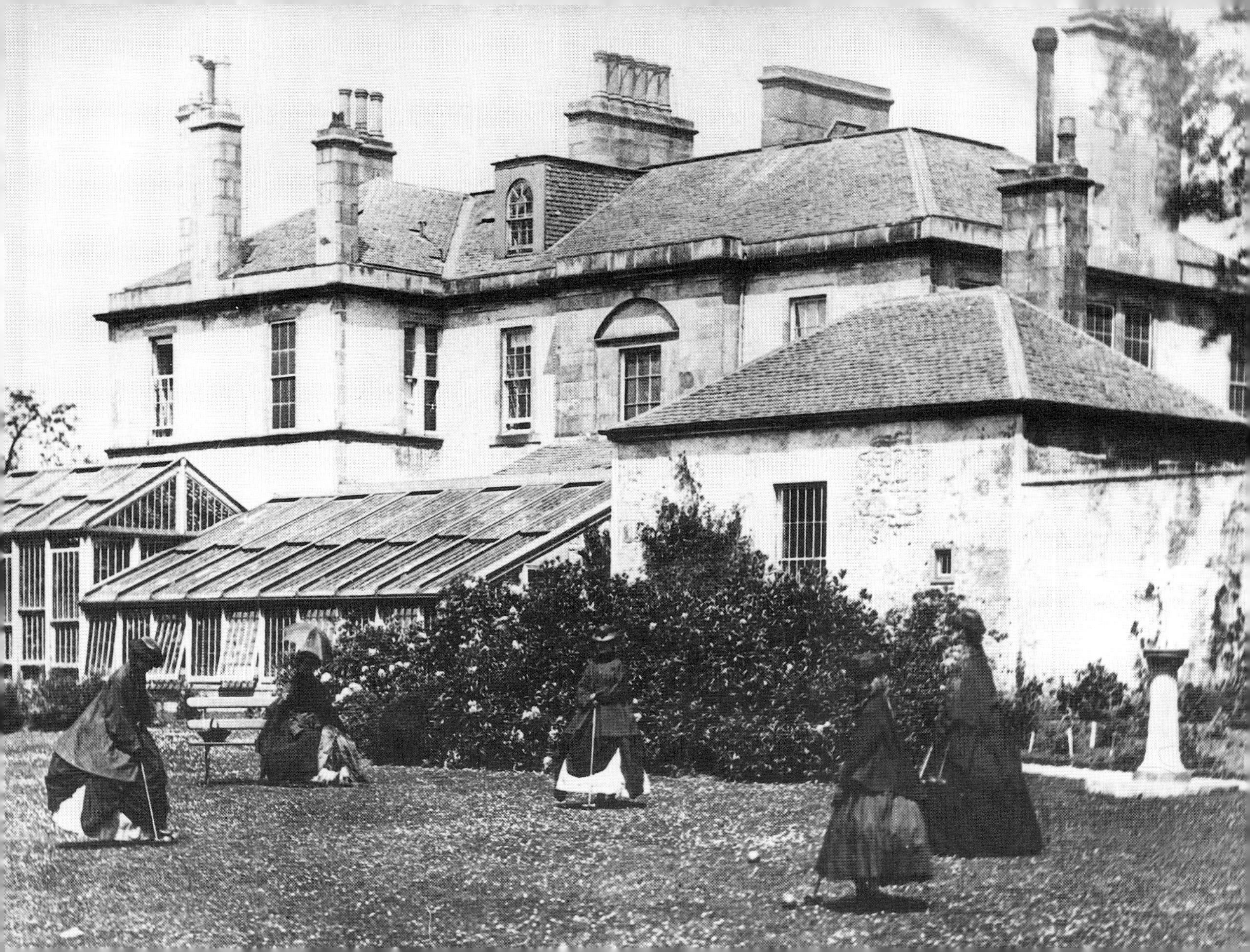

The stone-masons who built the house, C.1880

A LARGE TEAM OF TWENTY-FIVE STONE MASONS WERE EMPLOYED in building the house on Islay. Here assembled for their photograph, some of them have the tools of their craft in their hands and the most elderly of the company have been given the place of honour, at the centre, in the front row.

Many of them may have relatives alive today. Technological developments this century have given architects freedom to create new forms with new materials, but all must share a concern that important skills, such as those of the stone mason, should not be lost. These skills would not be easily reacquired and who can say that the quality of good stone-work may not enhance the finest contemporary buildings and those in the future.

It is right that the names of these men should be remembered:

From left to right, back row: William Morris, John Spalding, Andrew Campbell, Hugh May, Neil MacNaughton, Donald MacLugash, Angus MacCuaig and Donald MacNab.
Middle row: Charles MacKinnon, John MacInnes, John MacGinty, John MacMillan (Jnr), Donald MacGilvray, Donald MacArthur, James Campbell and John MacCallum.
Front row: John MacMillan (Snr), Robert Black, Donald Spalding, James Muir, David Meldrum, Duncan MacCuaig, Adam Calderwood and James MacCalman.

It is thanks to the thoughtfulness of the owner of the property that this visual and verbal record exists.

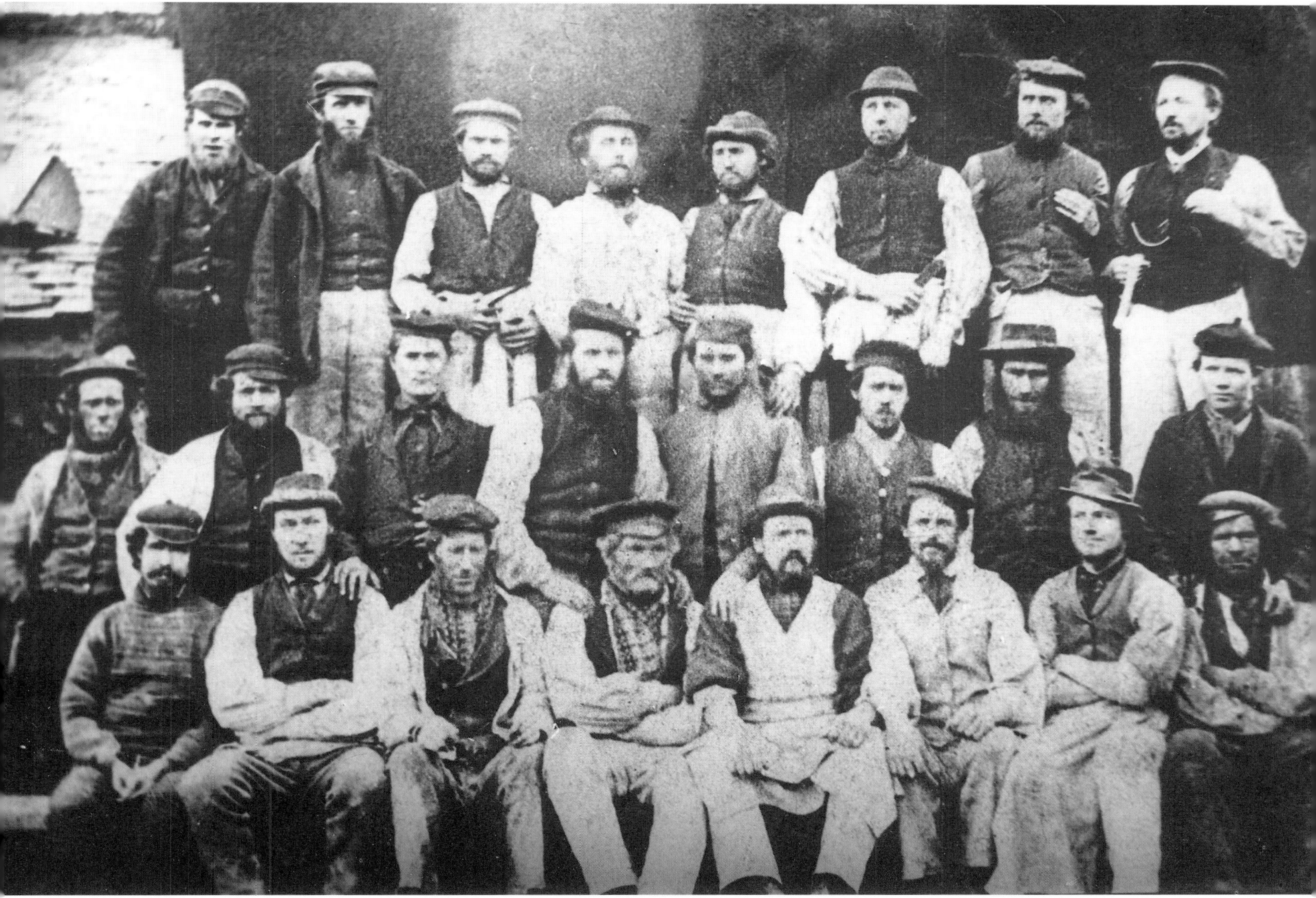

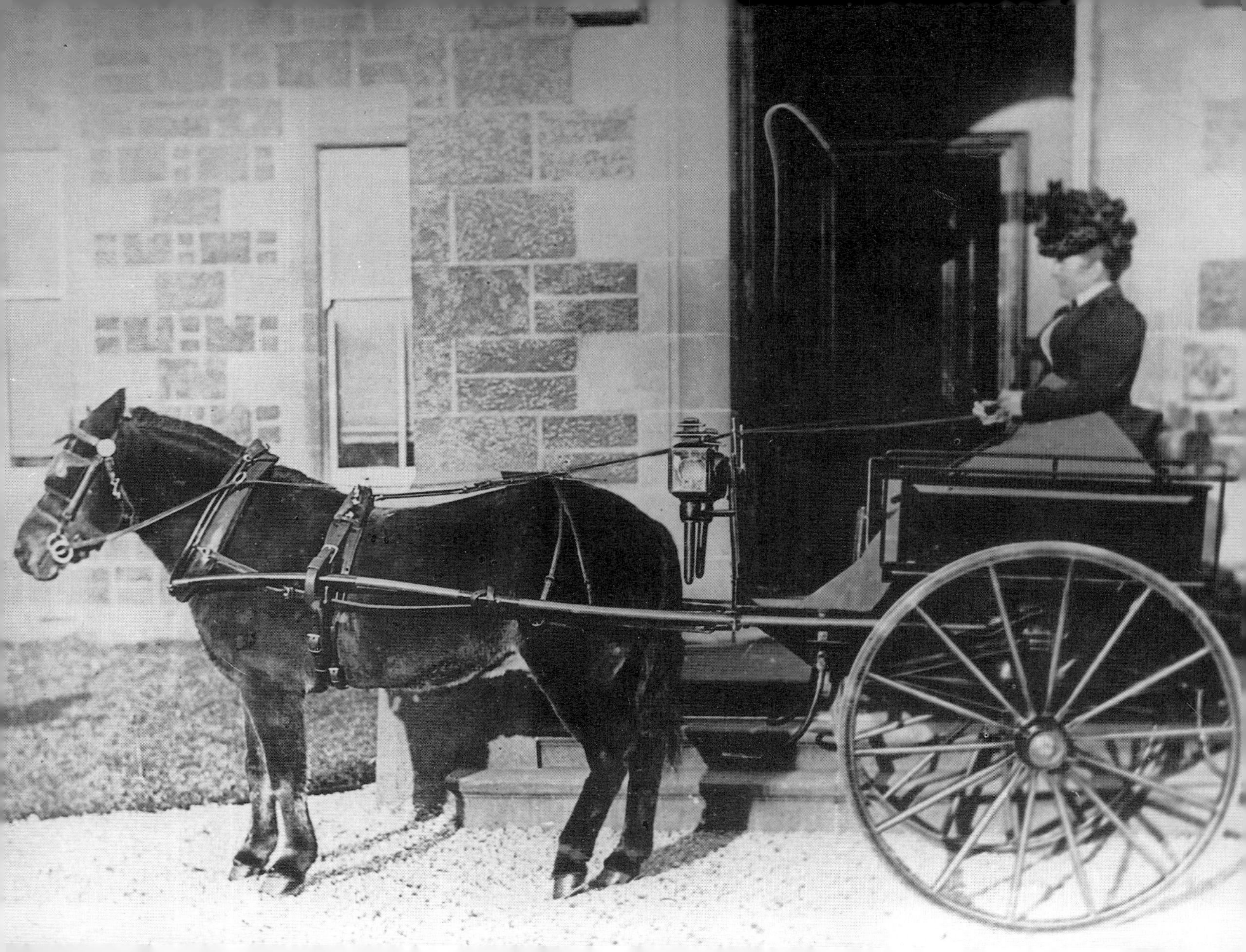

A lady setting out to pay a call C. 1890

WHAT A SMART TURN-OUT! THE HOGGED MANE OF THE PONY and the polish on her hooves, the light, spick-and-span vehicle with its brilliantly shining candle lamps and the large, spotless leather apron, as well as the lady's hat and clothes all indicate a visit on which there will be no difficulty about reserving 'a trot for the avenue'. What an example of the wheelwright's art are those slender-spoked light wheels shod with thin, solid-rubber tyres, the ultra light shafts and the beautifully polished harness. It all has the lightness, balance and perfection of:

> *The wonderful one-hoss shay,*
> *That went to pieces all in a day.*

One cannot see this vehicle travelling very far over rough island roads. We are reminded too of how much of a lady's time was spent in making and receiving calls and leaving cards. The fact that she is driving herself is a reflection of island living, indicating informality, a low traffic density and, in all likelihood, a short journey. In those days, she is very likely to have been entertained on her arrival with a glass of Madeira and a slice of Madeira cake, a plain cake which was specially designed to be enjoyed in this way.

Madeira cake

This excellent classical cake, intended for eating while enjoying a glass of Madeira, should be served absolutely plain, never given a filling of any kind and a caraway seed should not be allowed within an ass's roar of it. Seed cake is quite another and a coarser story.

> *100g caster sugar*
> *275g white self-raising flour*
> *100g vanilla sugar*
> *4 whole eggs, well beaten*
> *200g butter or vegetable margarine*
> *25ml milk*
> *a small pinch of salt*

Set the oven to pre-heat to 180°C. (350°F.) Gas Mark 4 and prepare a 30cm diameter cake tin, preferably one with a detachable bottom, by lining it with a round of baking paper cut to fit the bottom and a strip to go around the inside. Cream the butter or margarine with the sugars in a large warm mixing-bowl until they are smooth and evenly incorporated, then, alternately, sift in the flour and add the well beaten eggs, adding only a little of each at a time, finally slowly mix in the milk. Spoon the mixture carefully into the lined cake tin, making sure that there are no cavities left and bake on the middle shelf of the oven for 35 to 40 minutes, keeping a watch that the top does not get beyond a rich golden colour and testing with a thin skewer to ensure that the inside is cooked. Have ready a wire rack, take the cake from the oven and leave it in the tin for 5 minutes before turning out onto the wire rack. When cold keep in an airtight tin.

Grandsons of the House, C. 1912

O<small>N THE SURFACE THIS IS A CONVENTIONAL SCENE, BUT THERE ARE</small> interesting disparities. The boys are fitted out for the occasion but observe their mounts' condition and particularly their hooves, which are unshod and unpolished. No very serious amount of riding is taking place here as may be seen from other indications as well. The dogs look truly contented and that fussy self-importance shown by some spaniels is amusingly illustrated. It is high time the boys were being taught to look after their animals better. Perhaps they could be persuaded to go off and gather rowan berries for the cook to make that most delicious conserve for eating with meat, rowanberry jelly.

Rowanberry Jelly

1 Kg ripe rowanberries
4 large cooking apples
1 Kg pectin-coated sugar
cold water nearly to cover the fruit

Remove every particle of stalk from the rowanberries, as stalks tend to make the jelly bitter. It is all to the good if a few yellowy-green unripe berries are present as they increase the pectin and, as long as they do not form more than a proportion of one in fifty they will not spoil the flavour.

Simply quarter the apples, leaving peel and cores. Put berries and apples into a large saucepan with just enough cold water not quite to cover the fruit and bring to the boil. Boil rapidly for an hour, then turn all the liquid and fruit pulp into a suspended jelly-bag and leave to drip overnight.

Next day, squeeze the jelly-bag gently but firmly to expel the last of the juice, which is richest in pectin, measure the quantity of juice and transfer to a large, thick-bottomed saucepan or preserving-pan.

Prepared in this way, a kilo of berries should yield one litre of juice. For each litre of juice add one kilogram of sugar, i.e. equal unit volume/equal unit weight.

Heat the sugar and the juice slowly together in the saucepan, stirring continuously with a wooden spoon, making sure that every grain of sugar is dissolved before the juice reaches a boil. Once you are certain that the last grain of sugar is dissolved, the heat can be increased, but will need to be reduced when boiling commences to prevent an over-boil even in a deep saucepan.

As soon as a rolling boiling is well established, set a timer for 8 minutes (in spite of what they say on the packet of sugar). After 6 minutes (this time applies only if you are using pectin-coated sugar) test a few drops for setting on a cold plate. When a set takes place take off the boil and allow to stand for a couple of minutes and skim any froth from the top before bottling and sealing, while hot, in sterilised jars.

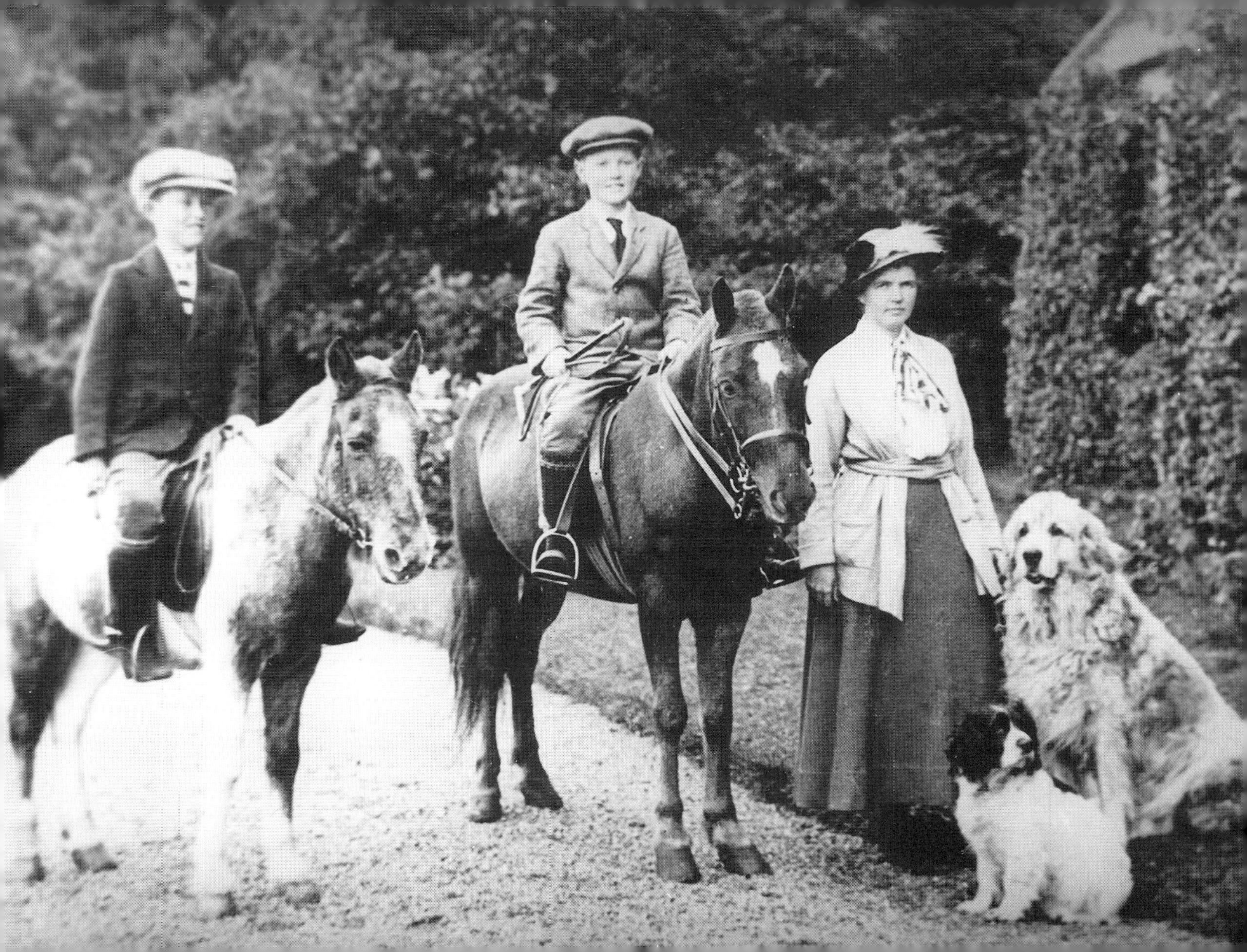

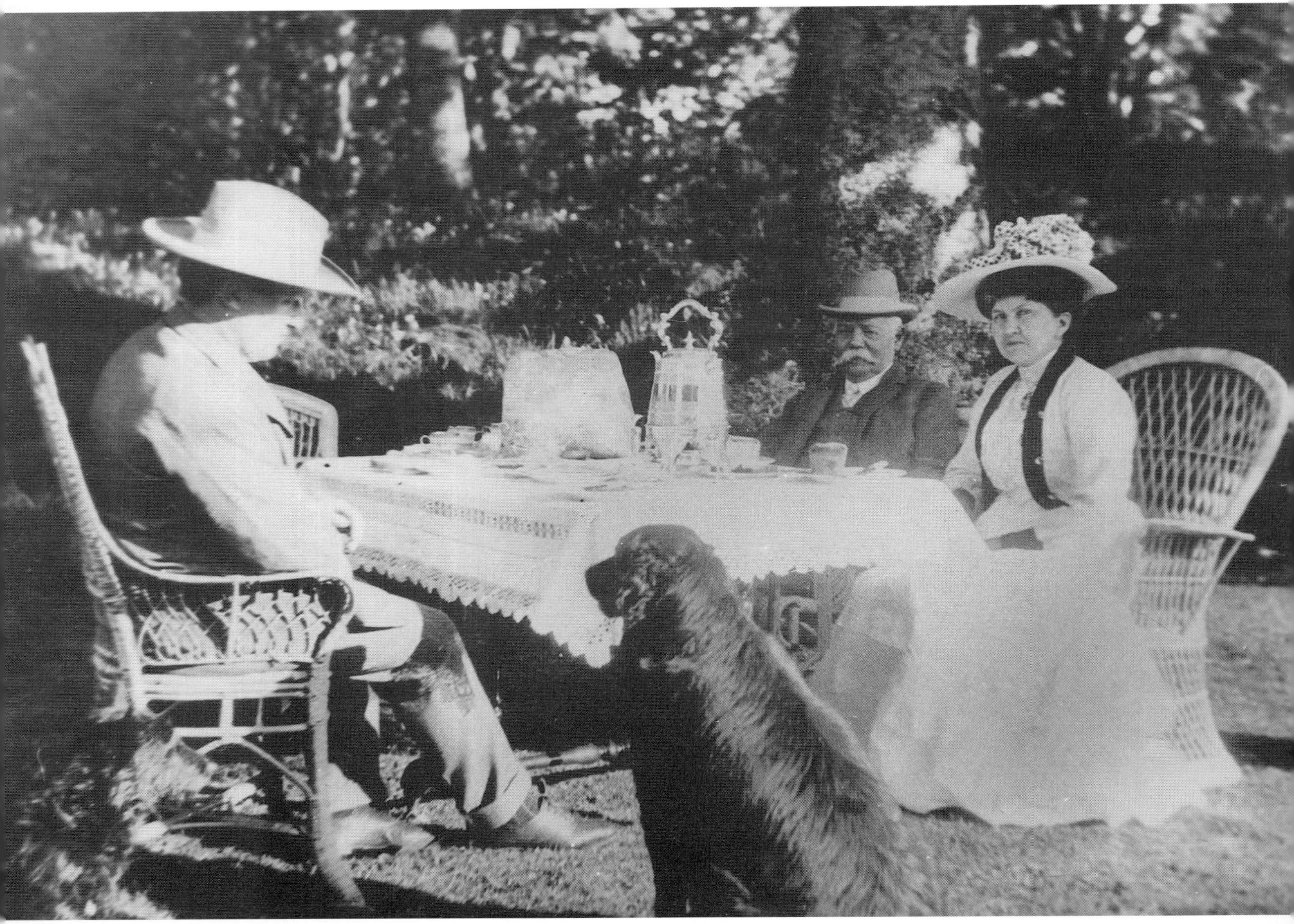

Afternoon Tea in the Garden, C. 1910

The final touch to the domesticity of this scene of afternoon tea in the garden, where all the period apurtenances are present in the form of spirit-lamp heated hot-water kettle, cosy-clad teapot and drawn-thread-work tablecloth, is provided by the presence of the retriever, whose figure shows us clearly that this is not the first occasion of the kind she has attended. It would seem that past experience has taught her to address her attentions to the son of the house and we hope that, the photograph taken, her patience will have been rewarded, though there is an indication, in the absence of a cake dish, that the tea has been a frugal one. Retrievers who have acquired the habit of afternoon tea are so inclined to lose their figures, particularly if they have a liking for some of the delicious confectionery of the Scottish kitchen such as Tantallon Cakes.

Tantallon Cakes

225g sifted white wheat flour
225g caster sugar
225g sifted rice flour
2 whole eggs, beaten
1 level teaspoon bread-soda (bi-carbonate)
finely grated rind of 1 lemon
225g butter
a little caster sugar to garnish

(Yield: around 15–20 small cakes according to size.)

Mix well the two flours and the bread-soda. Cream the butter and the sugar with a wooden spoon in a warm bowl. Beat the eggs and add in small amounts at a time, alternating with the mixed flours, sifted in, in small amounts at a time, beating well between each addition. Lastly, evenly work in the finely grated lemon peel and mix all thoroughly. Pre-heat the oven to 200°C. (400°F.) Gas Mark 6. Put the dough onto a lightly floured pastry slab, roll out thinly and cut into small rounds, preferably with a scallop-edged cutter. Put the rounds onto a lightly greased baking-sheet keeping them about 5cm apart and bake for about half an hour until the tops are lightly golden. Cool them on a grid. When cold, powder them lightly with a little caster sugar.

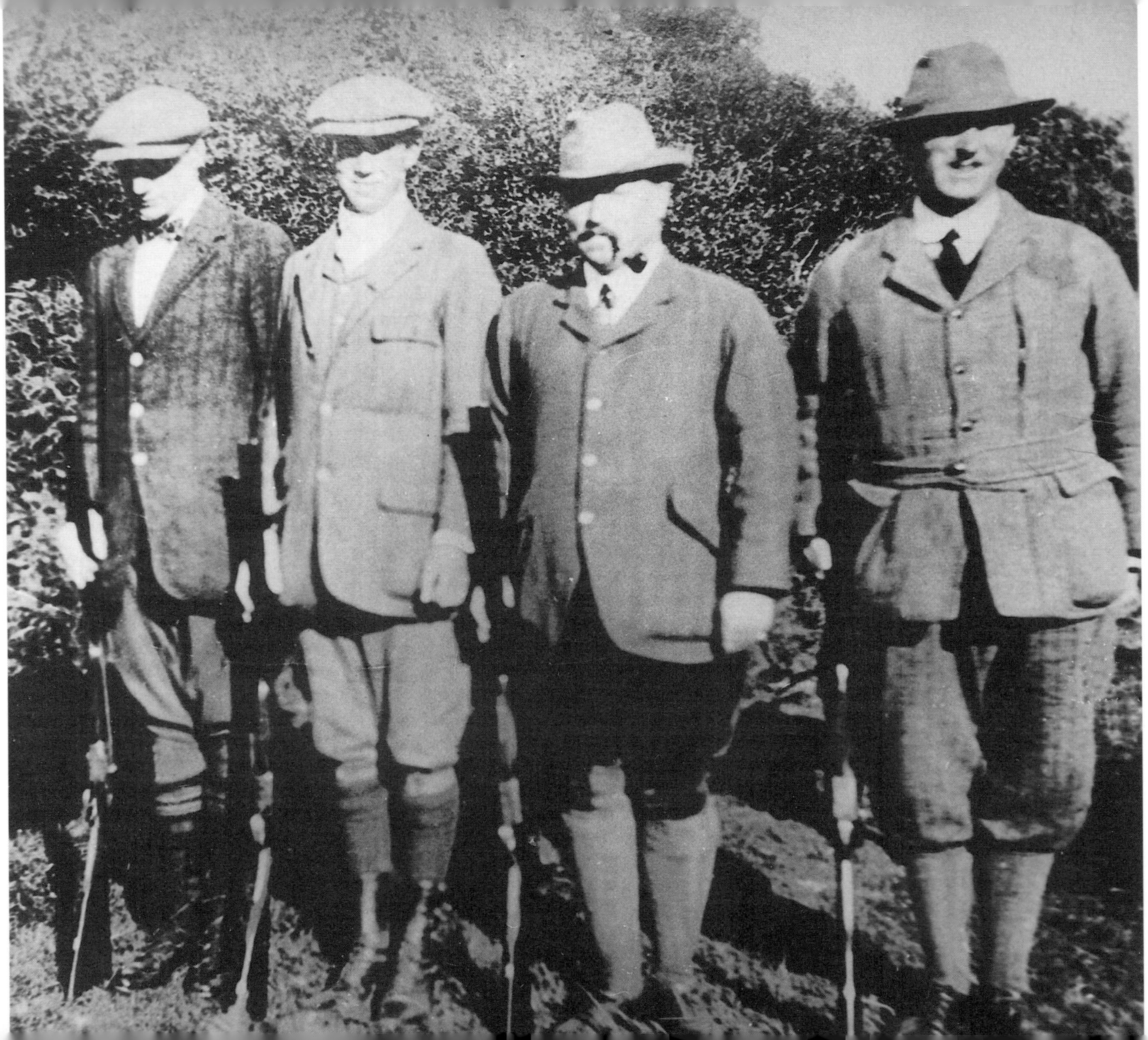

A shooting party, C.1900

Although the commercialisation of grouse-moors and other shoots had been taking place for some time when these sportsmen lined up for their photograph, there were, and still are, many private shoots remaining. The wild game of Scotland is proverbial, drawing enthusiasts from all over the world.

Now it is no longer merely an interest in blood-sports, naturalists, both professional and amateur and environmentalists are appearing in ever increasing numbers and the importance of overall conservation of this precious inheritance has become a question of primary importance. When this group was taken, the view was that, in general, the wild fauna were not endangered and could be relied on to renew themselves without the assistance of man. Today we are more knowledgeable and wiser, realising that a careful measure of control is the only way to preserve a unique amenity, that can be endangered not only by over shooting, but also by the depredations of acid rain, radioactivity and other pollutants coming, often, from great distances, as well as the depletion of the ozone layer. Today we realise that our eggs are all in the same basket; the planet! Wild game is indeed a wonderful heritage and should be treated with the gastronomical respect and knowledge that it deserves. Here is a fine treatment for a saddle of hare.

Roast Saddle of Hare.

1 saddle of hare
4 tablespoons of cooking oil
75g moist Demerara sugar
85ml port, warmed
Salt and freshly milled black pepper
150ml game stock
A good handful of parsley, finely chopped
50g rowanberry jelly
1 shallot, peeled and very finely chopped

Pre-heat the oven to 190°C. (375°F.) Gas Mark 5. Rub the joint all over with the sugar, salt and pepper. Strew the chopped parsley and shallot in the bottom of a deep roasting-tin, lay the joint on top and paint all over with oil with a pastry brush. Put a sheet of kitchen-foil, shiny side up over the joint and roast for 1½ hours, then bring the port to a little below boiling, remove the foil from the joint and pour the hot port over it. Return the joint to the oven and roast for a further 15 minutes, frequently basting with the pan juices. Test with a fork for tenderness and remove the joint on a hot dish to a warm oven while you reduce the pan juices by half and add to them the rowanberry jelly (see page 60). Give a final taste for seasoning and pour the sauce into a hot creamer and serve with the joint.

Al fresco lunch and a pipe, C. 1914

Before the First World War, shooting, as distinct from hunting, tended to be very much a male sport, for women's clothes were only just becoming practical enough for them to participate without inconvenience in activities that took them, on foot, across country. Things were about to change in a sudden way that can hardly have been anticipated in the conversation of these two gentlemen; but even if they had an awareness of coming events, it was a widely held opinion at the time that, if war came, it would be over by Christmas. The big shoot was about to begin. It would last much longer than anticipated and there would be no closed season.

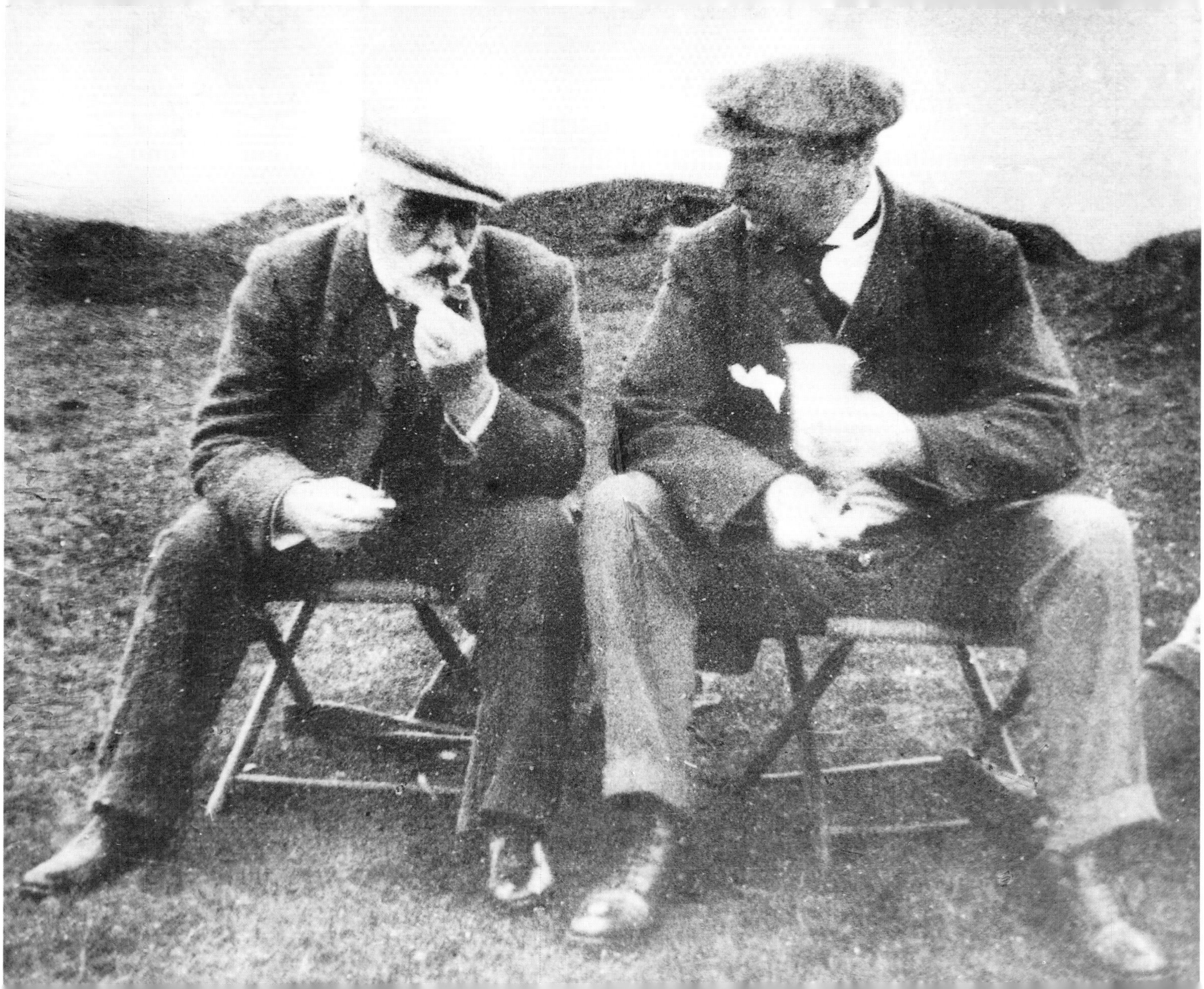

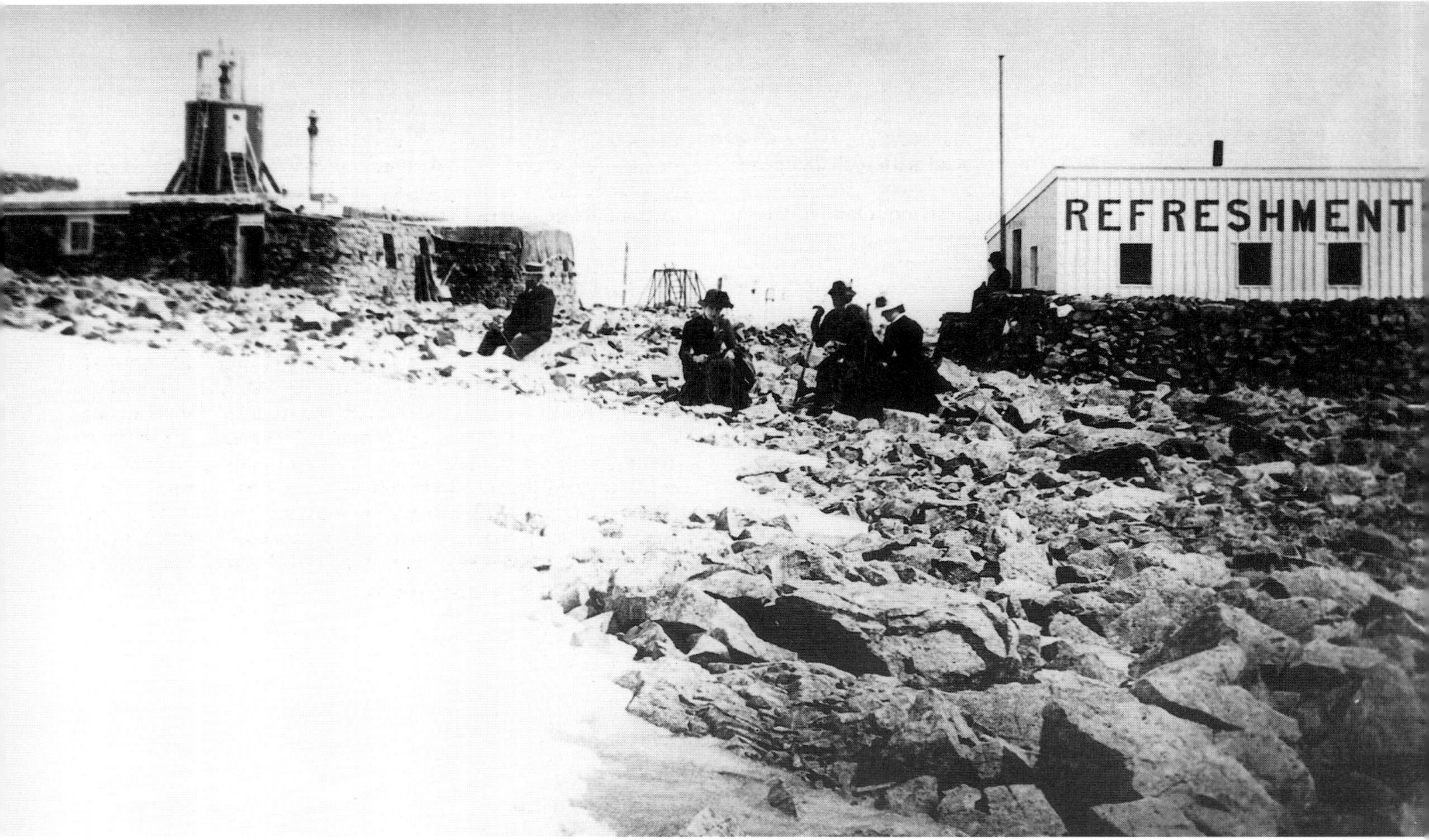
REFRESHMENT

On the top of the Ben, C. 1890

OUR HYPOTHETICAL GROUP OF TRAVELLERS MAKING A CLOCKWISE tour of Scotland would now be faced with a challenge of no mean dimensions.

Ben Nevis, at 1340 metres the highest mountain in these islands, being both higher and further north, carries its snow more continuously than Snowdon, at 1080 metres, and unlike the latter, has no railway to bring visitors to its summit in an enclosed and heated carriage; in the 1890s however it could boast both a licensed restaurant and an extensive weather-station there. Although essentially a walk-up mountain, it can be dangerous in places in fog and low cloud, so a good summer day is the best time to set out and early too, for it is quite a long and, at times, a steep and stony walk for which the right shoes are essential. On the west coast of Scotland, the weather can change with great suddenness, so a forecast of stable conditions is also desirable. It is advisable to carry with one supplies of both food and water as the steep parts of the ascent are thirsty work and one is not always conveniently near a burn. These conditions being fulfilled, the walk is an interesting one, though even on the best days one can never be absolutely certain that there will be clear visibility at the top, as in fine weather the peak still makes quite a bit of its own adiabatic cloud. Even on a calm day the top can be very windy. Don't make your climb in a picture hat. Don't forget, too, to leave plenty of time for the descent so that it is concluded before darkness begins to set in.

Ladies of the 1860s and 1870s must have found their clothing a considerable hazard during the climb and a hat-restraining tether as used in hunting would have proved serviceable to the gentlemen in the tall silk hats which the customs of the time demanded even on an expedition such as this, for in the 1860s the 'deerstalker' had not yet made a general appearance. The ladies in this photograph, although carrying considerably less 'canvas' than their earlier sisters and not encumbered with hoops, must have found the going none too easy. It is plain that the day of the photograph must have been exceptionally calm, as a straw boater needs only a very moderate breeze to convert it suddenly into a frisbee.

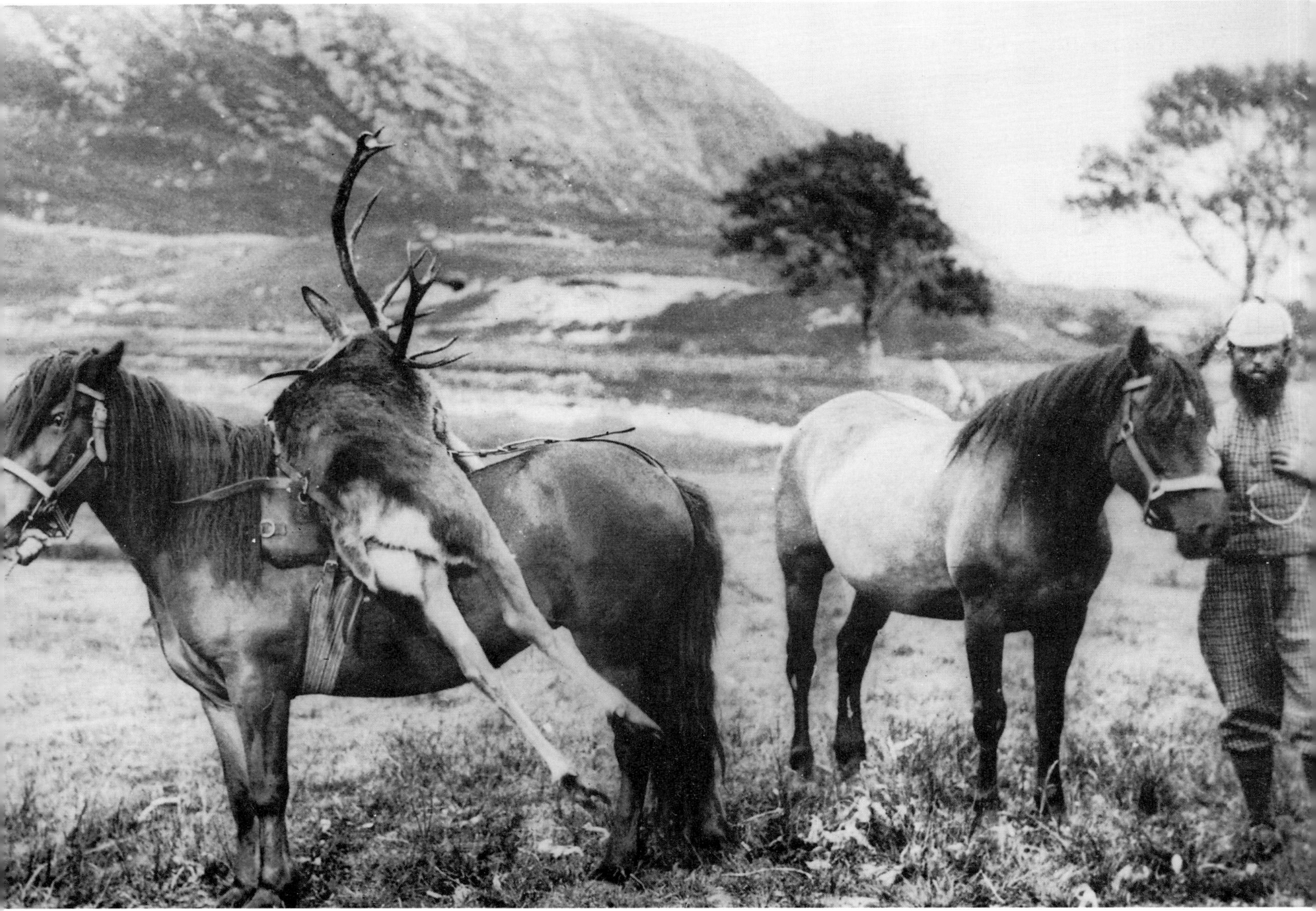

A stag from the Royal Forest of Glen Etive, C. 1880

THE MAGNITUDE OF THE CRUELTY INVOLVED IN STAG-HUNTING has convinced many today that it should be abolished as a sport, but the humane culling of these magnificent animals by professional marksmen under the control of zoologists who have the responsibility for seeing that the general health of the herd is protected, is a biological necessity, which can also provide supplies of that most delicious meat, venison. Perhaps only the wild boar, no longer found in these islands, can provide us with a gastronomical experience comparable in excellence. Out of respect for the magnificent animal one is about to eat, a certain degree of extravagance, if it is possible, should be considered. Here is another of my family recipes.

Haunch of Venison Morrison

Take a good thick haunch of venison, preferably of roe deer and well hung. Pour two bottles of dry white wine into a deep dish or large oval casserole with a lid. To the wine add two thinly sliced shallots, three good sprigs of lavender, finely chopped, and two crushed bay leaves. Put the joint into the marinade and if not covered by the wine turn it about several times to ensure that it is well moistened. Put the lid on the dish and set to marinate in a cool room, turning the joint about five times in 24 hours if the marinade does not cover it. To cook, pre-heat the oven to 190°– 200° C. (375°– 400°F.) Gas Mark 5 depending on the size of the joint. Put 4 tablespoons of a light cooking-oil such as Flora into a large roasting-pan (in the original recipe this was lard but the substitution does not impair the finished flavour and is better for our cholesterol levels). Put a grid into the roasting-pan to raise the joint well above the bottom, lay the joint on the grid, pour half the marinade over it and roast for 3–4 hours (or 25 minutes per half kilogram), meanwhile heating the remaining marinade to boiling and keeping it hot. Baste frequently with the pan-juices and with the remainder of the hot marinade and make sure that the joint does not get dry through excessive cooking. When it is done place on a hot dish and keep hot while you de-oil the pan juices in a creamer and combine them with the marinade adding a liberal tablespoon of rowanberry jelly. Reduce rapidly on the hob to half the volume, stirring vigorously. Serve in a sauce-boat with the venison. For the recipe for rowanberry jelly see page 60.

The Steam-Yacht Lancer, C. 1905

Fully to enjoy the west coast of Scotland it is necessary to take to the sea. Some rich families had their own steam-yachts, such as this one, at Oban, to bring them to and from their estates on the islands as well as for cruising. The period 1890–1914 was the hey-day of the privately-owned, screw-propelled steam-yacht. As the efficiency of the marine steam turbine required large installations, far larger than could be accommodated on board these vessels, they were nearly all powered by compound reciprocating engines and were almost exclusively coal burners. A great deal of attention was lavished by the designers on the appearance of the owner's accommodation by the use of fine woods, bevelled glass and luxurious fittings. The majority of these vessels were, however, not intended for use in heavy weather in an open seaway and the *Lancer* is seen to be no exception to this general rule. Some of the larger steam-yachts of the period were quite capable of ocean voyages, but the majority were more suitable for use in sheltered waters. They made ideal vehicles for expeditions among the archipelagos of the west coast where their manoeuvrability and reasonable turn of speed could insure that they were able to make a sheltered anchorage in good time if heavy weather threatened. For this reason the officers and crews were carefully chosen for their knowledge and experience of the complex systems of tides, currents and the other hazards with which these intricate waters abound. The awning fitted at the stern reminds us that, in those days, too much sun was regarded as injurious, an attitude to which we are wisely tending to return as the ozone layer continues to offer less and less protection. A party of congenial friends embarked on one of these vessels enjoyed one of the greatest recreations possible and even some of the most luxurious power-boats of today, in spite of their superior performance, lack something of the cachet of the old steam-yacht and many of them tend to be 'surface-skimmers' which depend greatly for their safety on their high power to weight ratio so that a run main-bearing in a remotely handled engine in a bit of a sea would make one very glad to have an efficient radio in operation. Modern power-boats, yachts and small fishing-boats account for the majority of life-boat calls.

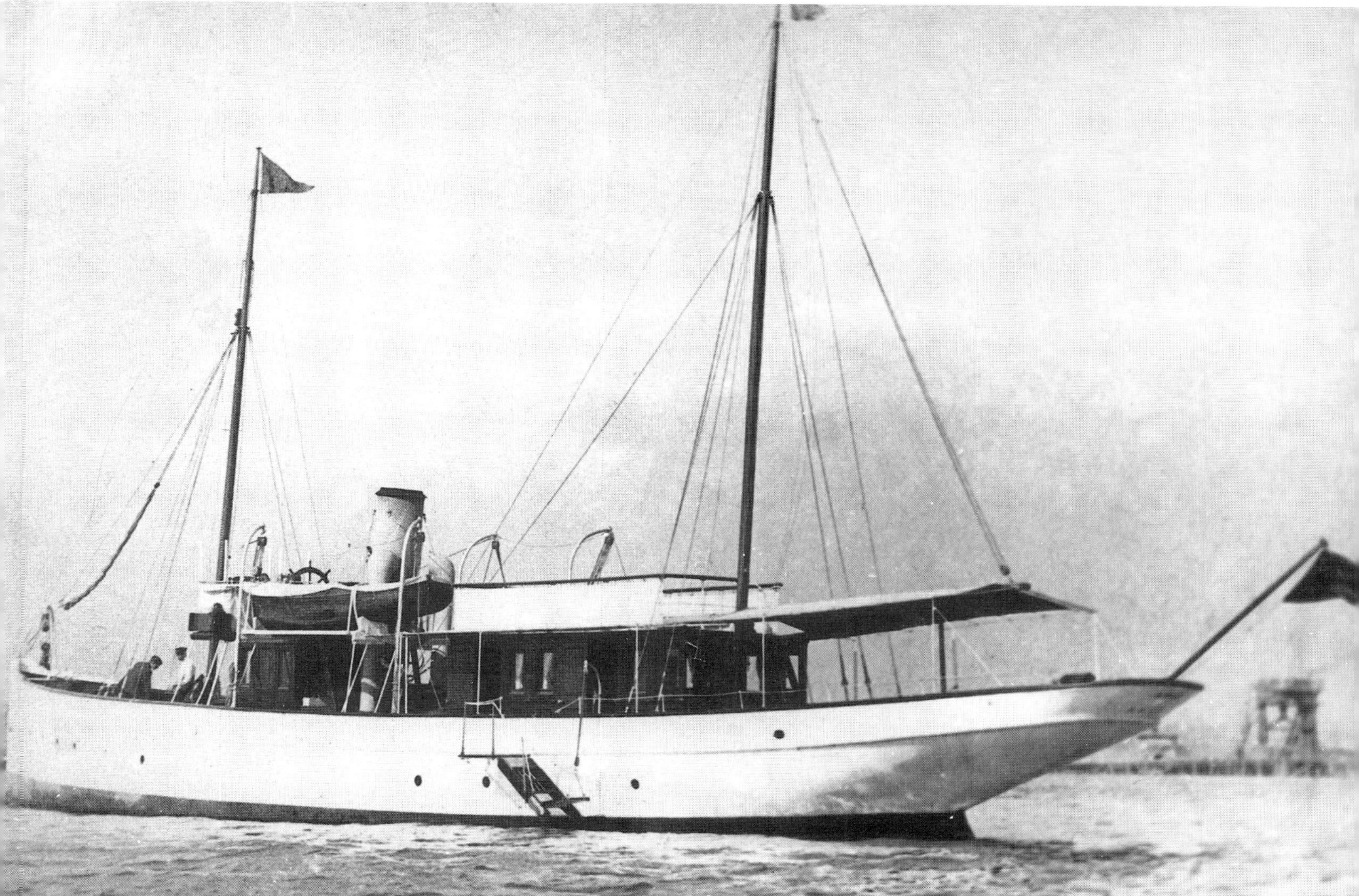

On board the steam-yacht Lancer, *C.1910*

STEAM-YACHTS WERE NOT BUILT FOR SPORT, BUT FOR THE enjoyment of Epicurean pleasures and as a convenient and comfortable means of transport. So far as their internal fittings were concerned, comfort they certainly did have. For one thing, they had in their cabins considerably more headroom than in most power-boats of today, which made the accommodation more airy and elegant. One cannot have it every way with a ship and the designers of the period recognised that the vessels would not, in general, be obliged to spend too much time in harsh conditions and this principle is readily seen in the construction of the *Lancer*. The guest who is amusing himself with a lady's parasol, clearly shows by his dress that he does not expect to experience much spray or sea-water coming over the low bulwark and the vessel's owner, seated on the rail of the flying bridge, is obviously of a similar frame of mind.

As one would expect at the time, the *Lancer* has no vestige of anything resembling a radio aerial and, once having left port, the company aboard would be out of communication until they put in to the next port of call. We need not commiserate with them as we can be pretty sure that all that they might desire could be found on board and their needs administered to by a well trained steward and an experienced chef, while the 'holy-stoned' cleanliness of the deck speaks of the conscientious attentions of the deck-hands. At sea, exposed to the wind, it is no bad notion slightly to increase ones calorie intake so here is a delicious Scottish boiled pudding.

Melrose Pudding

225g white self-raising flour
50g ground almonds
2 whole eggs, beaten
150ml milk
125g butter or margarine
50g halved glacé cherries
75g sugar

With a little of the butter or margarine lightly grease a pudding-basin that has a snap-on lid, then sift the flour and beat the eggs. Cream the butter and sugar in a warm bowl with a wooden spoon and when smooth add, alternatively, a little flour and a little of the beaten eggs, mixing well all the time. When these have been fully incorporated, gradually add the ground almonds and the milk in the same way, until the mixture is just still liquid enough to drop from the spoon. Stick the halved cherries by their flat sections to the sides and bottom of the greased pudding-basin and pour the mixture carefully into the basin so as not to disturb the cherries. Put the snap-on cover on the basin and steam in a steamer for around 2 hours. Take from the steamer and allow to cool for a few moments to set the pudding, then turn it out onto a hot dish and keep hot. It is excellent with brandy (or whisky) butter or a wine sauce.

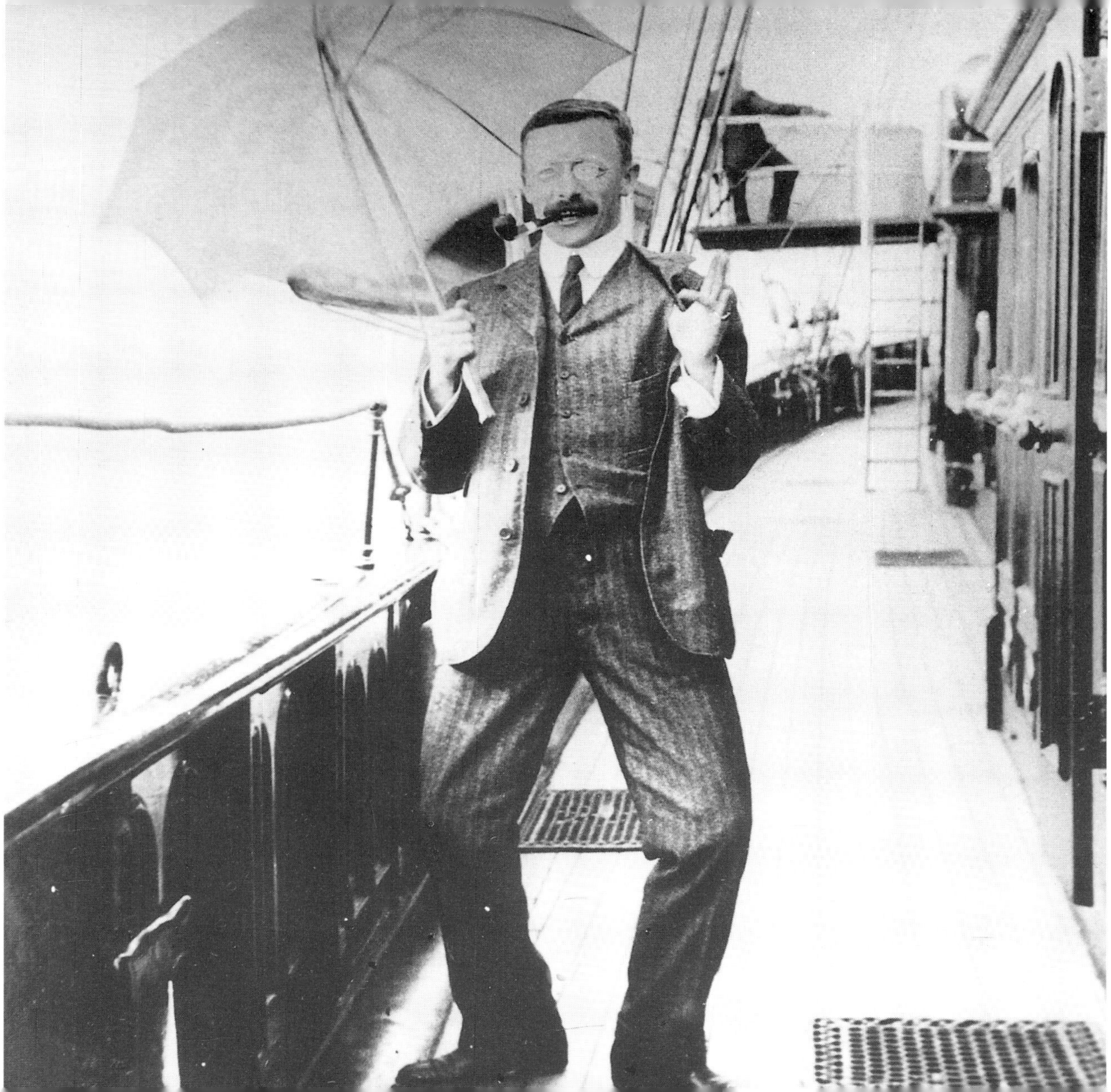

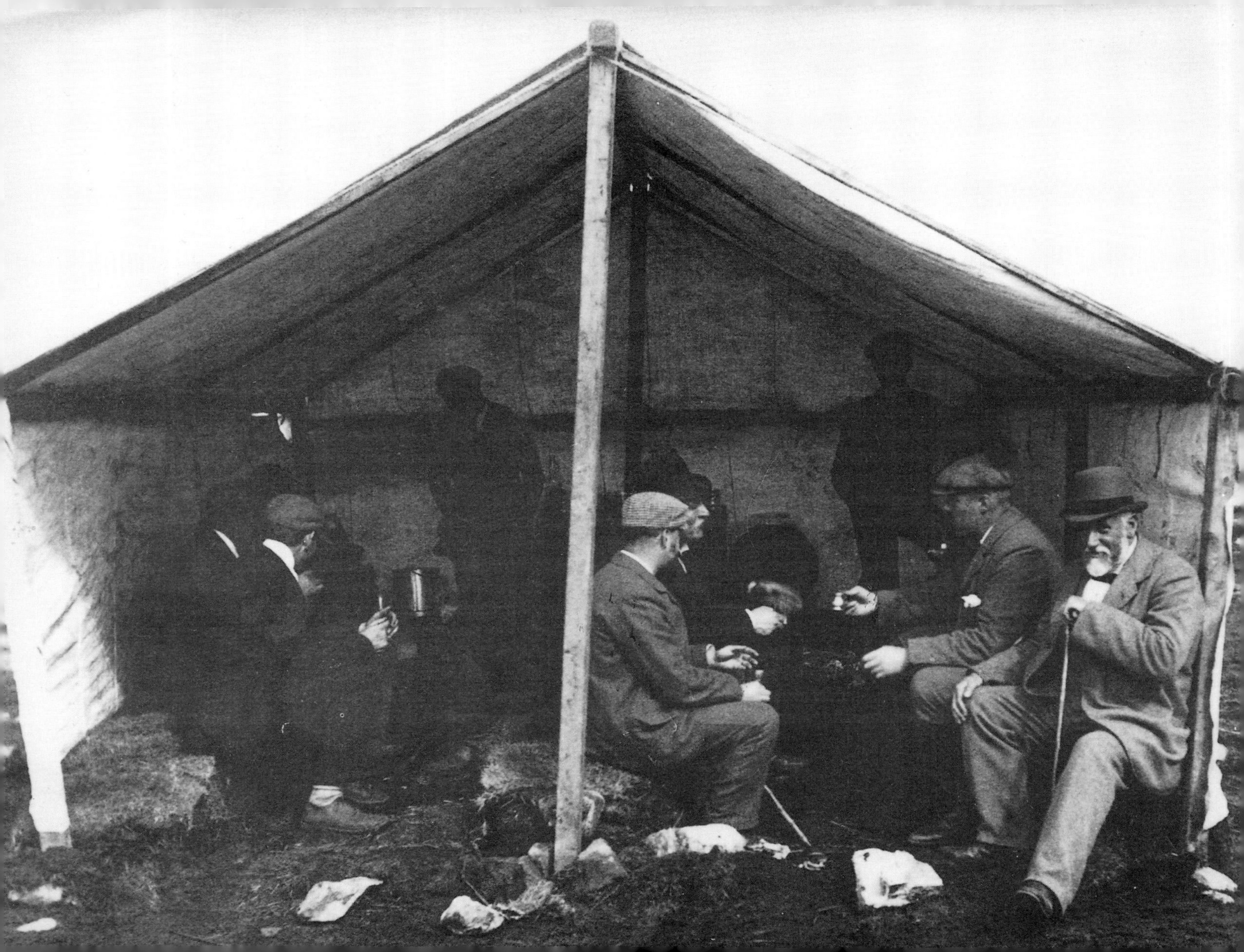

Fair Day on Benbecula. The refreshment tent, C. 1910

THE LONG ISLAND, AS THE OUTERMOST CHAIN OF ISLANDS KNOWN usually as the Outer Hebrides, lying further to the west and most exposed to the Atlantic are locally called, have an environment which is different from the inner islands, both in climate and people. More exposed to wind and storm, with few trees and a greater proportion of heather and bog, there is much less agriculture and a greater emphasis on sheep raising. The people of 'The Long Island' are different too, for here is to be found an area where the Norse element has remained strong and where descendants of the two most Norse of the Scottish clans, the Macleods and the Morrisons are still to be found. The Macleods trace their descent from Norse Kings of Man and the seat of their Chief is Dunvegan Castle on Skye, the Morrisons from a party of Vikings from Norway, wrecked on the Butt of Lewis, which is the reason why the badge of their clan is 'driftwood' to this day. A family of this Clan were for centuries hereditary deemsters of Lewis.

Being more isolated than most of the other islands, ten miles of water separating the closest point, North Uist, from Dunvegan Head on Skye and Stornoway, the capital, being well over three hours by ferry from Ullapool, the inhabitants are more thrown back on their own resources.

Here, on the shore on Benbecula, one of the middle islands in the chain, the annual fair is in progress and the refreshment tent is well patronised. One of those present is enjoying his 'dram', not from the traditional 'quaich', the small silver or wooden drinking bowl with handles at opposite sides at the top, but from a common measure, several others of which stand on a shelf at the back of the tent. It is clear from the clothes seen that the day was not a cold one, but if it had been otherwise, it is probable that a toddy would have been on offer.

Toddy

3 or 4 lumps of sugar
boiling water
a generous slice of lemon with the peel on
150ml milk
whisky, hot but not boiling

Put the sugar into a toddy-glass, rummer or other suitable glass and place in it too, a silver spoon. It is best to use a silver spoon as the very high thermal conductivity of the silver prevents the glass from cracking when the hot water is poured into it. Pour enough boiling water over the sugar so that it dissolves, then add an equal amount of hot whisky, crush the lemon to release the juice, stir well and there you are.

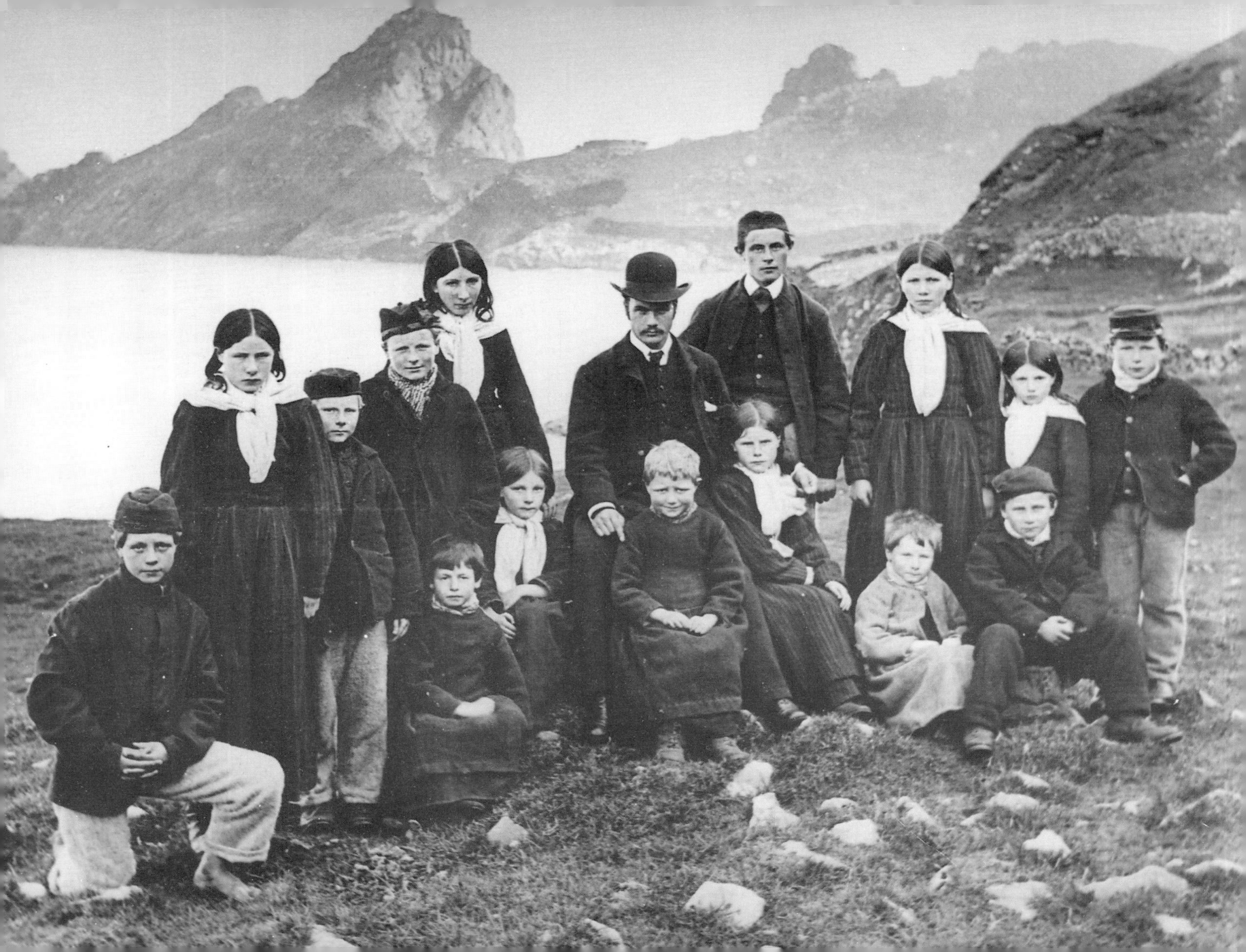

The schoolmaster and his pupils, St Kilda (Hirta), 1880s

IF OUR TRAVELLERS HAD AVAILABLE TO THEM A VESSEL SUFFICIENTLY large and seaworthy, they would have been able to enjoy an unusual experience not available to us today. Setting out from the Outer Hebrides and steaming nearly due west into the ocean for forty miles, they would have found themselves approaching the largest island of a small archipelago. St Kilda or, to give it its Gallic name, Hirta, the one inhabited island of the group. Such an expedition would only have been possible in the summer months for, except for a small landing-place on the south east, cliffs, rising almost sheer from the ocean reach, in places, over 300 metres high and to go ashore there is only practical during four months of the summer due to the inadequacy of the landing-place and the swell of the ocean. People lived there, until quite recently, at least from Viking times and the unusual social pattern developed is a legacy from the Northmen, although Gallic was the spoken language. The pattern of life that existed when this photograph was taken somewhat resembled that of the Färoese, though because of the restriction of their safe access to the sea, fishing never seems to have been as prominent an activity. Education from outside came to them in the early 1880s, brought by a son of the island trained on the mainland, who was the first official teacher, here seen surrounded by his pupils.

For centuries the island had belonged to the Macleods and, though sold in 1779, it was bought back again by the Macleod of Macleod in 1871. Consisting largely of volcanic rock, the archipelago is thought by some to be the much eroded remains of an ancient caldera though sedimentary sandstones are also found, the strata of which show much tilting, as may be seen in the background of the photograph.

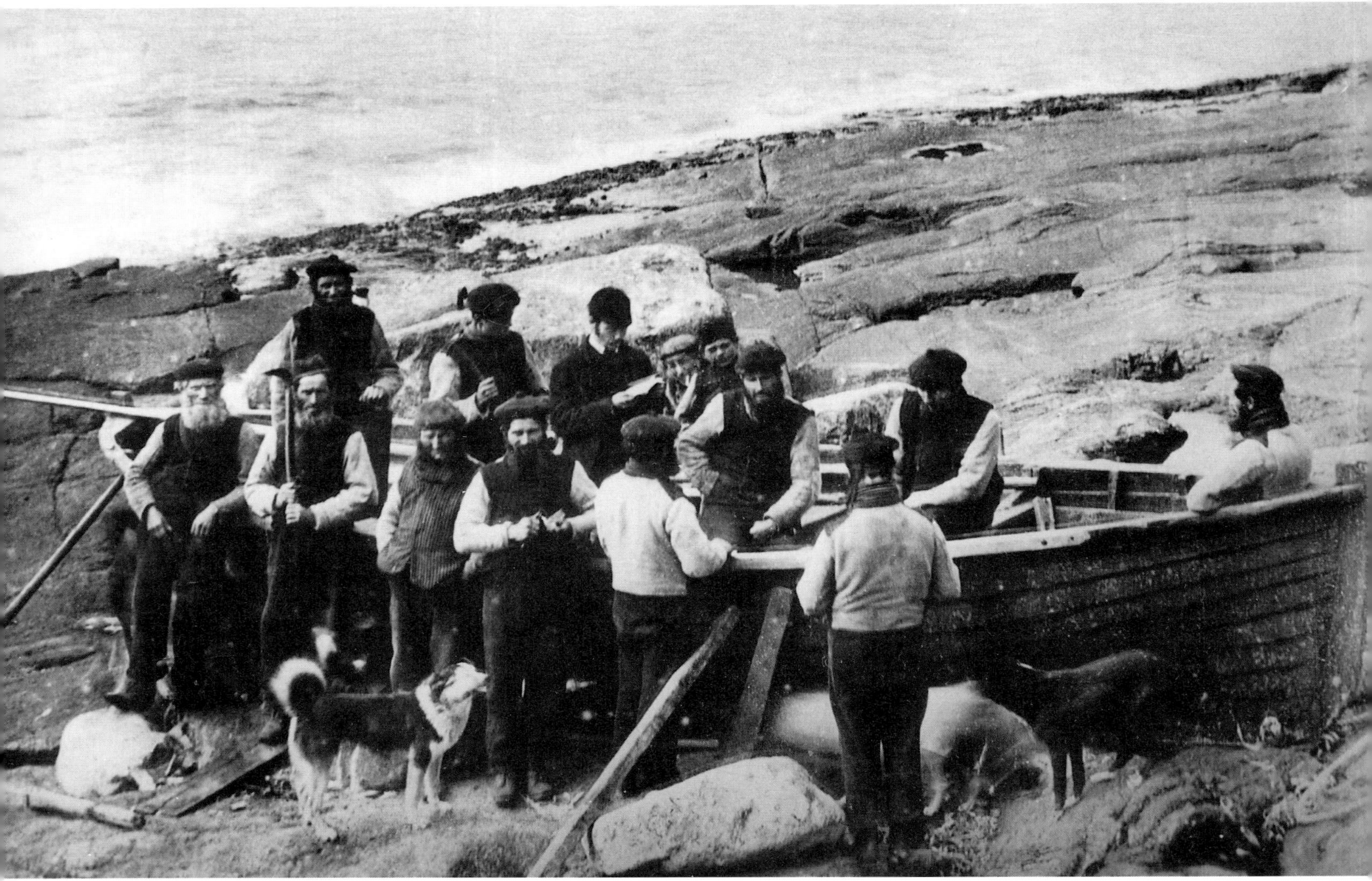

Men repairing the boat, St Kilda (Hirta), 1880s

Perhaps because of the Norse influence, the curragh type of boat so prevalent on the western islands of Ireland was not found on St Kilda. As there were no trees to provide timber, driftwood washed ashore was the only source of the materials for the repair of this clinker-built boat that was probably imported already built. The job of keeping it in repair is a communal one for the men of the island. The vessel was of great importance to them as a means of ferrying their sheep out to vessels calling during calm weather in the summer time and bringing ashore people and supplies from outside. So dangerous was the coast of the island that comparatively little fishing was carried out, but the dogs remind us that around a thousand sheep were raised each year. A few cattle were kept for milk and meat and on the forty acres of arable land were grown potatoes, oats and barley, but one of the most important sources of food to the St Kildans were the many sea-birds which made the island their breeding ground.

The chief catch was of young fulmars, but puffins, razorbills, guillemots and solan geese were also taken. These fish feeding birds were used by the islanders as a source of oil for their lamps as well as for their nutritive value. Most of their clothing was produced on the island from the wool of the sheep and rough leather jackets were also made but their boots appear to have been imported. In the middle of the group, the schoolmaster appears again, reading a book, but wearing a different and more suitable hat. The traditional hats of the men are clearly seen as are their sleeveless jackets of island-woven tweed worn over knitted woollen pullovers. As on the Färoes and Fair Isle, knitting was a winter occupation undertaken by both sexes. It is interesting to notice how the dogs have gathered sociably at the scene of work, their behaviour suggesting that they are on good terms with the men and not frightened of them, nor can they be accused of 'cupboard-love' for there is no sign of food about.

The islanders showed also a sign of Icelandic influence, being self governed by a 'parliament' consisting of a gathering of the male heads of families and under it all major undertakings were communally organised, reminding us that the democratic process in northern Europe today owes as much to the Icelanders as it does to the Greeks.

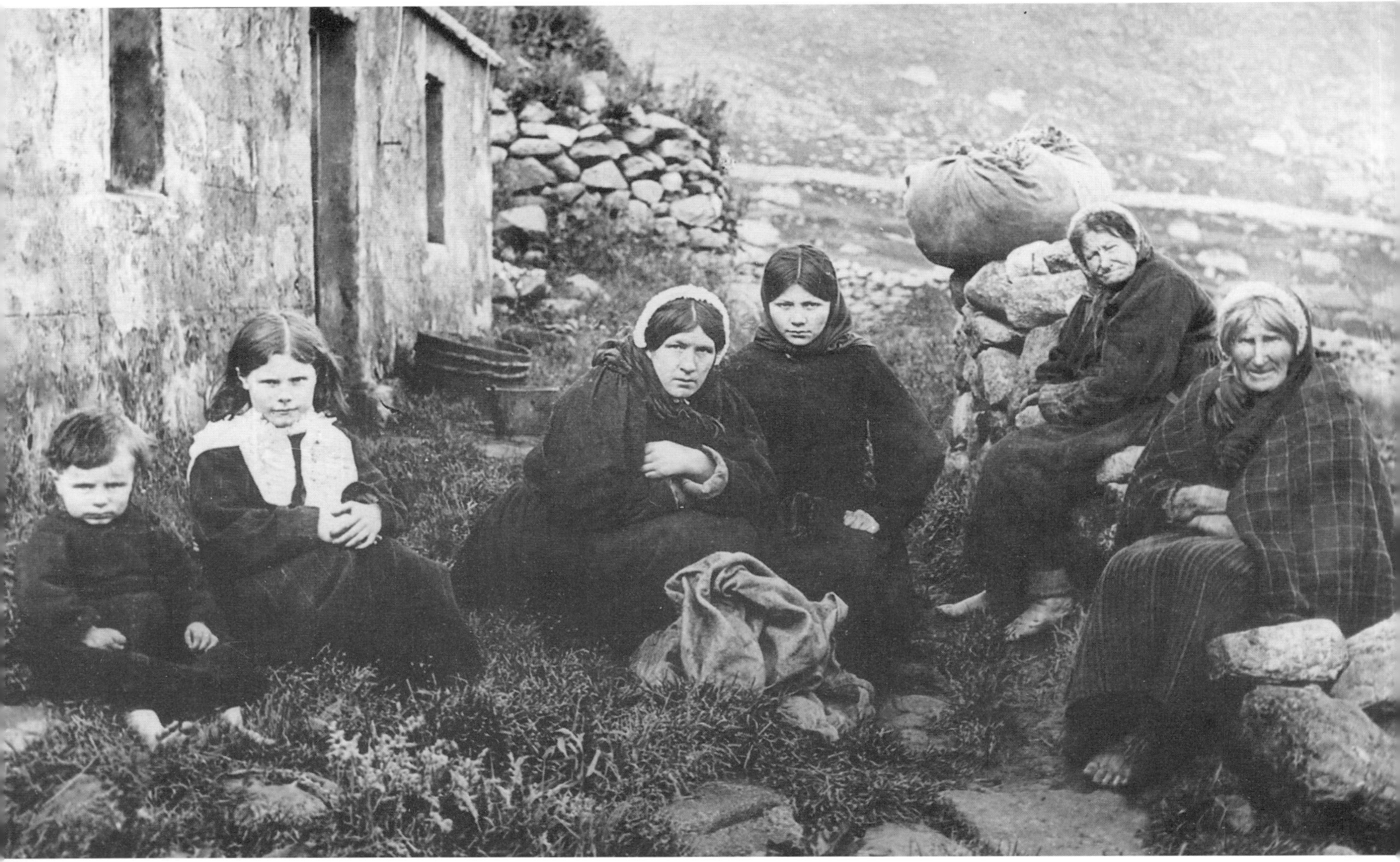

Women and children by an abandoned house, St Kilda (Hirta), 1880s

SHEARING OF SHEEP WAS NOT PRACTISED ON THE ISLAND. THERE was a more primitive system. The wool was removed from the sheep by plucking and then handed over to the women for washing, carding, spinning, bleaching and dyeing before being used either to weave into coarse tweeds or to make knitted garments. For the latter purpose the wool was used in its natural, unbleached, undyed state to take advantage of the water and damp resistant properties of the lanolin it contained, which also made it harder-wearing and longer-lasting as the fibres retained their flexibility better. Here the women and children have been engaged in washing the wool, making use of a partly unroofed, abandoned house for their work, for the size of the population was shrinking.

The community had been infected with smallpox in 1724 which decimated it, leaving only thirty survivors, yet so healthy and vigorous was the life of the people of the island that in a century and a quarter, despite the harsh conditions of life, there were 110 of all ages living there. From that time onwards, however, slow depopulation began, partly accelerated by the increase in contact with the mainland due to the development of steamships.

An exceptionally isolated community like this is enormously vulnerable to infection with viral and other conditions from which large communities are able to build up a degree of immunity.

'The Boat Cold', as it was called from the means by which the infection was brought to the islanders, was a powerful influence in reducing the vitality and numbers of the community and diseases such as measles and whooping-cough were real killers, as they were with the Inuit peoples.

One very significant disparity between the sexes is noticeable, fewer boots are seen among the women, who all have the healthy, sturdy feet of people who often spend hours without shoes, and the men must have done likewise for their feet show the same characteristics.

The elderly woman in the right foreground is wearing the characteristic woven tweed patterns of the island, and note the married woman's custom of wearing a small cap of undyed, knitted wool. In conditions of this kind, though protected from frost to an extent by the Gulf Stream, wind-chill is a hazard and this is reflected in the design of the clothing of women, children and men.

In such an exposed situation way out in the North Atlantic, the wind force in cyclonic depressions can often attain values higher than all but the most severe storms on land. The houses were carefully sited to give them the maximum shelter and were roofed with heavy slate flags 5cm thick. On Friday, August 29, 1930, the last of this community abandoned their island and settled on the mainland, ending more than a thousand years of island life.

Men sharing out the catch of fulmar, St Kilda (Hirta) C. 1880s

GANNET, PUFFIN AND GUILLIMOTS WERE TAKEN FOR FOOD ON St Kilda, but the bird most sought after by the islanders was the fulmar *(Fulmaris glacialis)*, a large petrel ranging the northern oceans and having one of its chief breeding stations on the island. This bird played a very important part in their subsistence economy for, after the considerable quantities of altered fish-oils which the flesh contained had been extracted for use in the islanders' lamps, the birds were air-dried, salted and smoked as a staple source of protein for the long winter months. The fishy oil, though having a strong, very tenacious smell and taste, was highly nutritious and formed an important source of vitamins A and D in the islanders' diet, for dairy products were deficient in quantity and quality though they did keep a few cattle.

The fulmar cull was communally organised and was restricted to a single week in August when immature birds only were taken, though in very large numbers. The operation entailed teams of men lowering rock-climbers by means of ropes of twisted horse-hair over the edge of the cliffs to reach the otherwise inaccessible ledges where the birds nested in enormous numbers. The young men of the island were not supposed to get married until they had each their horse-hair fowling rope and so would be able to feed their family. The catch was then, communally, divided up according to the size of families, the birds being sorted into heaps by the men while the women looked on, as we see in the photograph.

The birds were then plucked, cleaned and air-dried in 'stypes' or small houses built of and roofed with peat, the ends of which were open along the axis of the prevailing wind so that the birds were quickly dried, after which they were smoked and stored for winter eating.

The Vikings perfected the art of preserving food of different kinds by air-drying, smoking and salting. The prevalence of cold, dry polar air assisted this process in the same way that the cold dry alpine air assists the Swiss. It may be that these techniques were introduced to this community in Viking times. There being no trees, the community were dependent on driftwood for building and fitting stypes and for other repair work, so timbers of any size were far too valuable to be used as fire-wood and peat had to be dug and dried for fuel.

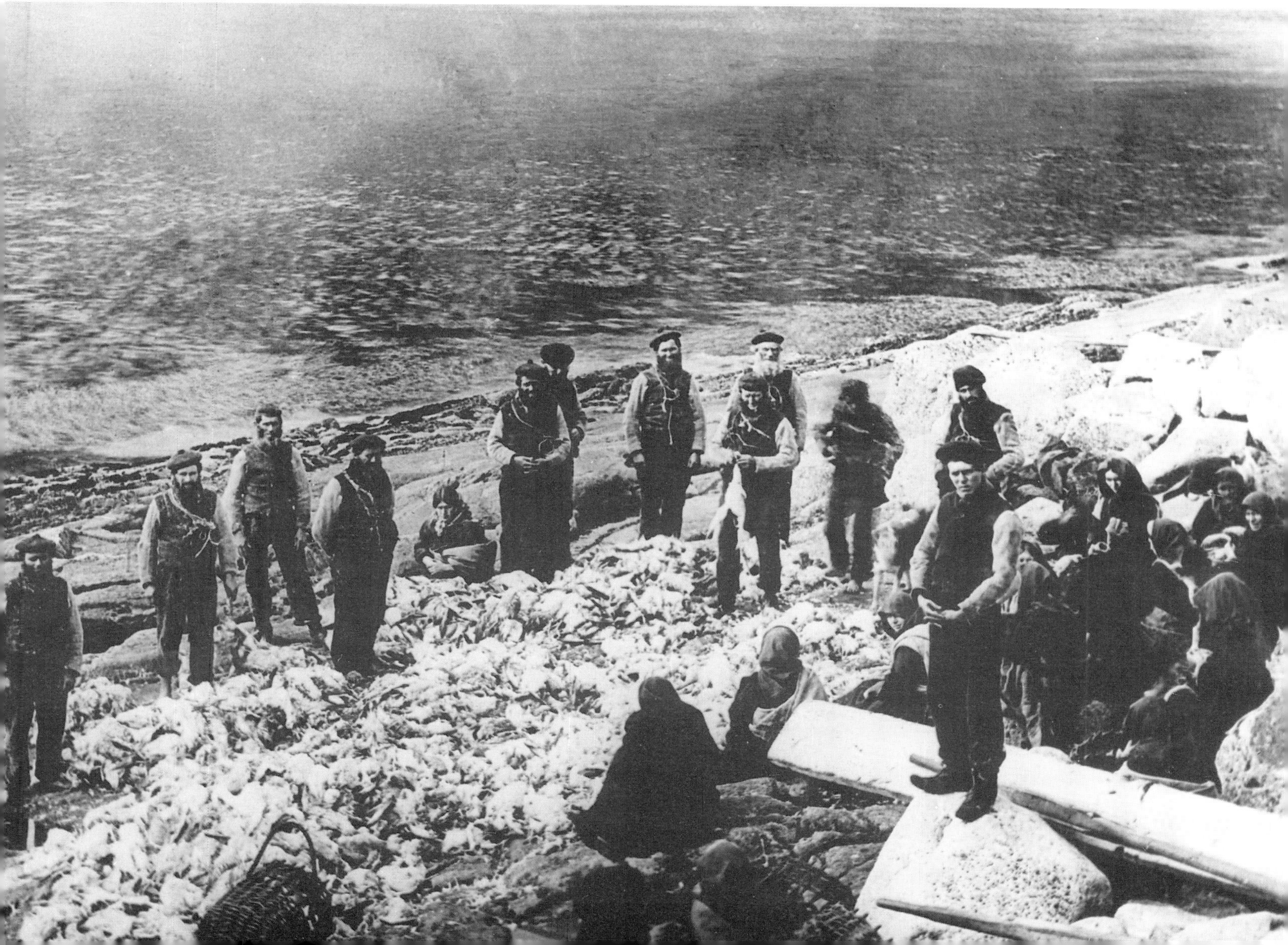

Women and children with home-spun and woven cloth drying. St Kilda (Hirta), 1880s

Here, in a sunny corner, sheltered by a dry-stone wall, a group of women have been busy knitting, but have stopped at the request of the photographer. They are using the undyed wool which is made into the woolly caps and sweaters. On the wall behind them are draped lengths of the island tweed, the prevailing patterns being well displayed, on the wall and on the woman to the right of the photograph. For the women, knitting was a year round-activity and clearly one which gave them the chance to get together and chat, particularly in the summer when working outside, in good light, was possible. In the winter evenings when the only light would have been from the fire and perhaps a cruisie filled with fulmar oil, more attention would have to be given to the work and in the small interiors, the numbers of women would not have been great.

We must hope that the weather was as kind to our party of travellers as it appears to be in these photographs, for otherwise they might have had to spend very much more time on the island than they would have bargained for before they could have got aboard ship and been brought back to continue their tour. Salted and smoked fulmar were the staple food of these islanders during the winter months, but a bird which they esteemed as a delicacy was the gannet or solan goose and indeed this fine bird (*Sula bassana*) was generally considered excellent eating until almost the beginning of this century. If you can lay your hands on one, the way to prepare it is as follows.

Braised Solan Goose

1 gannet, hung, plucked and trussed
bouquet garni of thyme, sage, lovage, lemon thyme, parsley and a crushed bayleaf
4 large carrots, scraped, cut into thin strips lengthwise
salt and freshly ground black pepper

Hang, pluck, draw and truss the birds as you would poultry. Wipe carefully inside and out, put into a large saucepan, cover completely with cold water and add the remaining ingredients, seasoning to taste. Bring slowly to the boil and simmer very gently (important, if boiled hard the bird will be tough) for two hours or until tender when tested with a fork. Allow the bird and the vegetables to get cold in the water overnight. Serve cold with a garnish of the vegetables or, if preferred, covered with a garnished *chaud-froid* made from the reduced stock.

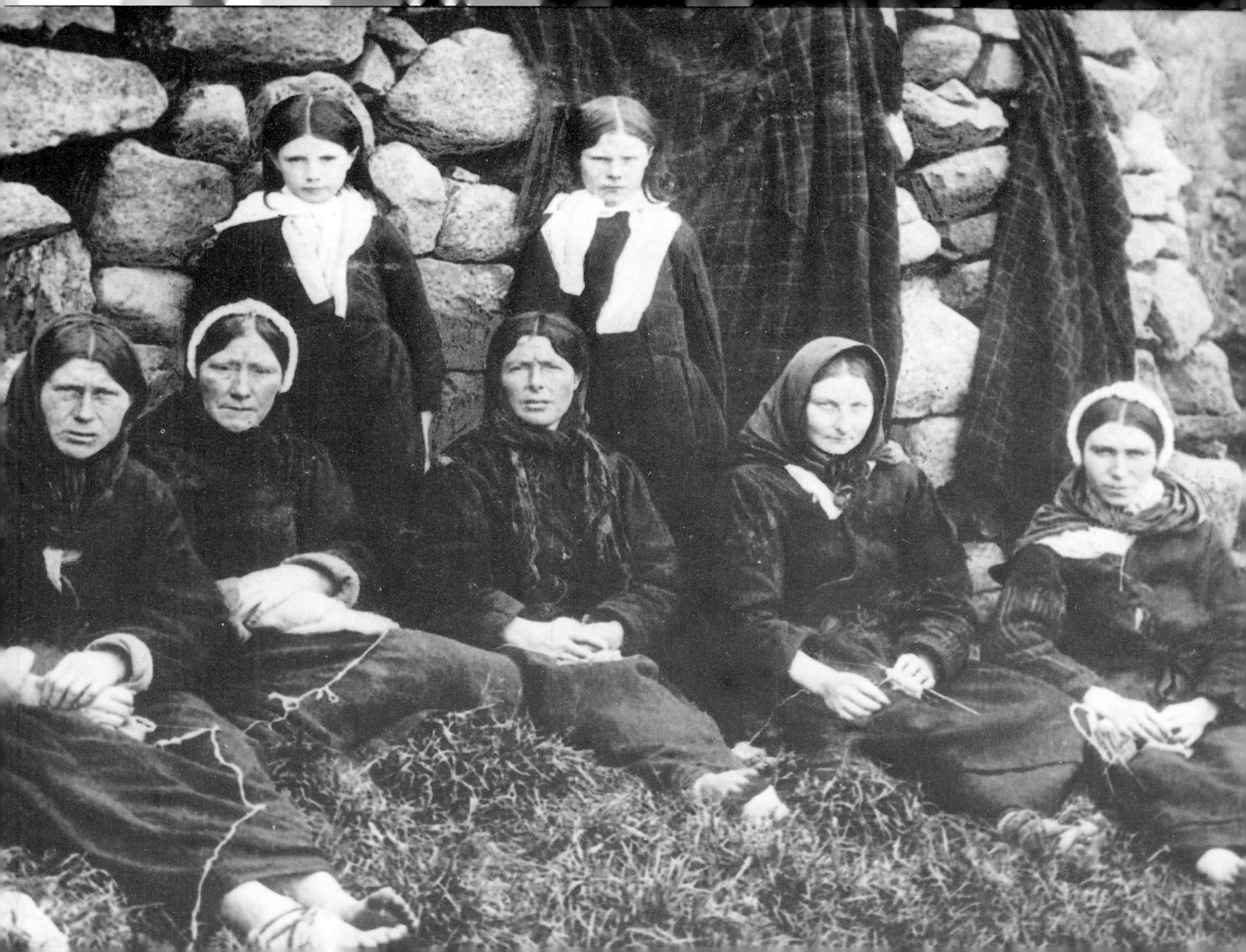

A lobster fisherman with lobster-pots, Kirkwall Harbour, Orkneys, C. 1900

Heading away from St Kilda on a north-easterly course to open and safely pass the Butt of Lewis and Cape Wrath, then steaming along the north coast of Scotland and through the Pentland Firth, our party would make for Kirkwall in the Orkneys.

The people of these islands, the chief seat of the Northmen's power in Viking times, have always lived by the sea as well as the land and the coasts of the islands have provided a habitat for one of the world's most delicious shellfish (page 12). Kirkwall Harbour with its long breakwater serves as an ideal base for this lobster fisherman pulling out to set his lobster-pots.

He must be anticipating very calm conditions outside, for even a small amount of swell would soon tumble his pile of pots over the side. Rowing around the coast to set his pots was much more tiring and hazardous than setting them from the powered boats of today. If the weather gave a sudden turn for the worse, he did not have the option of making a quick return to sheltered water but depended on his muscle power to get him to safety.

This is a good moment to consider the proper way to cook and prepare this magnificent shellfish. Studies at the Jersey Marine Biological Laboratory have shown that the kindest way of boiling a lobster is to immerse it in cold sea-water and bring it very gradually up to boiling-point in a closed pot with a tight-fitting lid, when the lobster faints away, as one would oneself in a Turkish bath if one stayed in it too long. When plunged into boiling water the lobsters were shown to suffer on average 58 seconds of agony and tense all their muscles, giving rise to a condition known as cadaveric spasm, which results in their being tough, nor can they be made tender subsequently if cooked in this cruel way. Kindness to lobsters is kindness to one's digestion. Once on the boil, cooking time should hardly be longer than for hard-boiling an egg and the lobster should be allowed to get cold in the water. Endeavouring to get the meat out of a cooked lobster with a hammer is a mug's game. First disjoint it, gently prising off the forelegs by bending against the resistance of the joints and giving sideways movements as you do so (don't forget to collect the juice that comes out as you do this), then, with side-to-side movements and a steady gentle pull, separate the tail from the thorax and abdomen. The individual sections can then be easily clipped open with a pair of side-cutters and all the meat and curd removed completely, even the claw meat intact. Split open the body with a strong knife and a mallet.

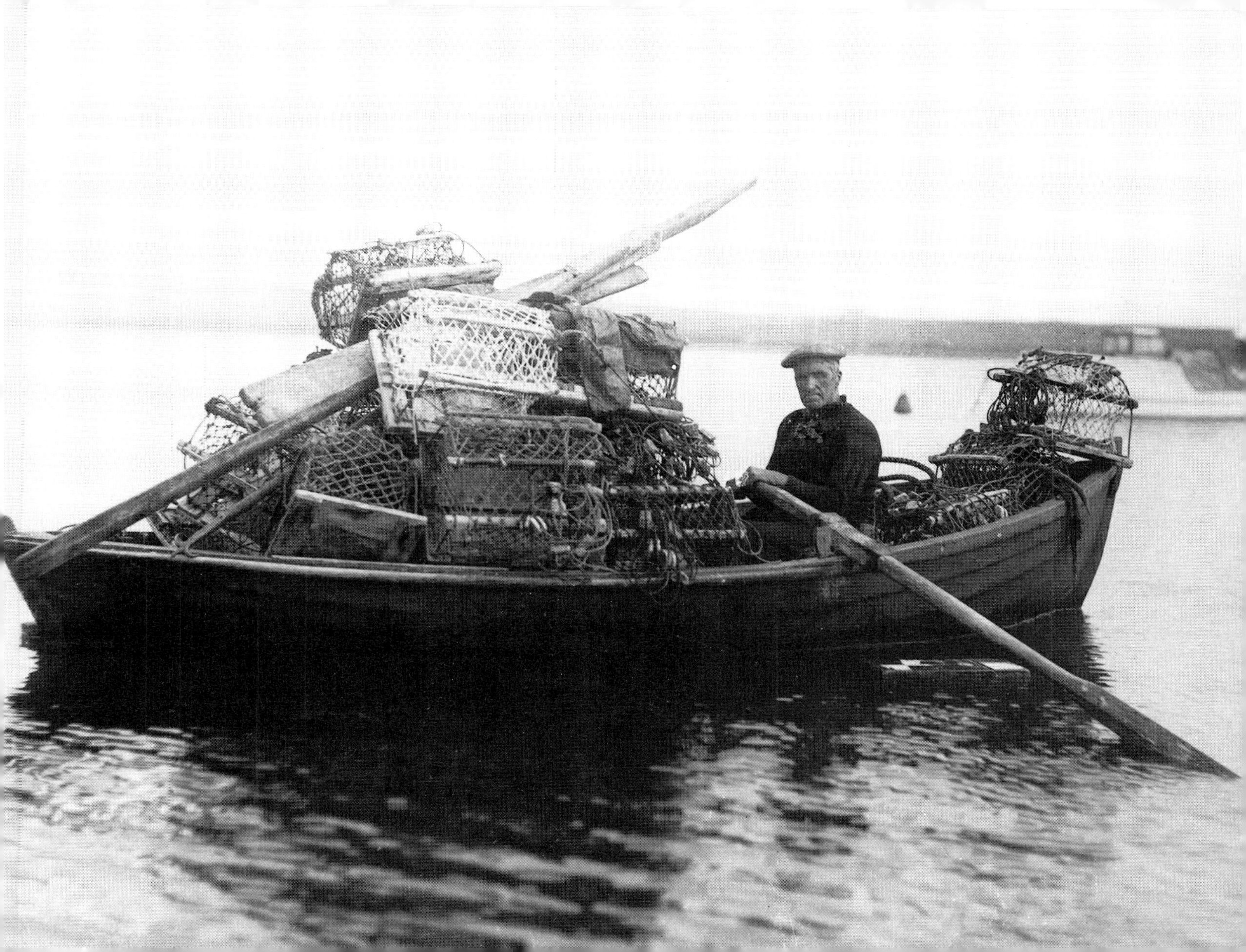

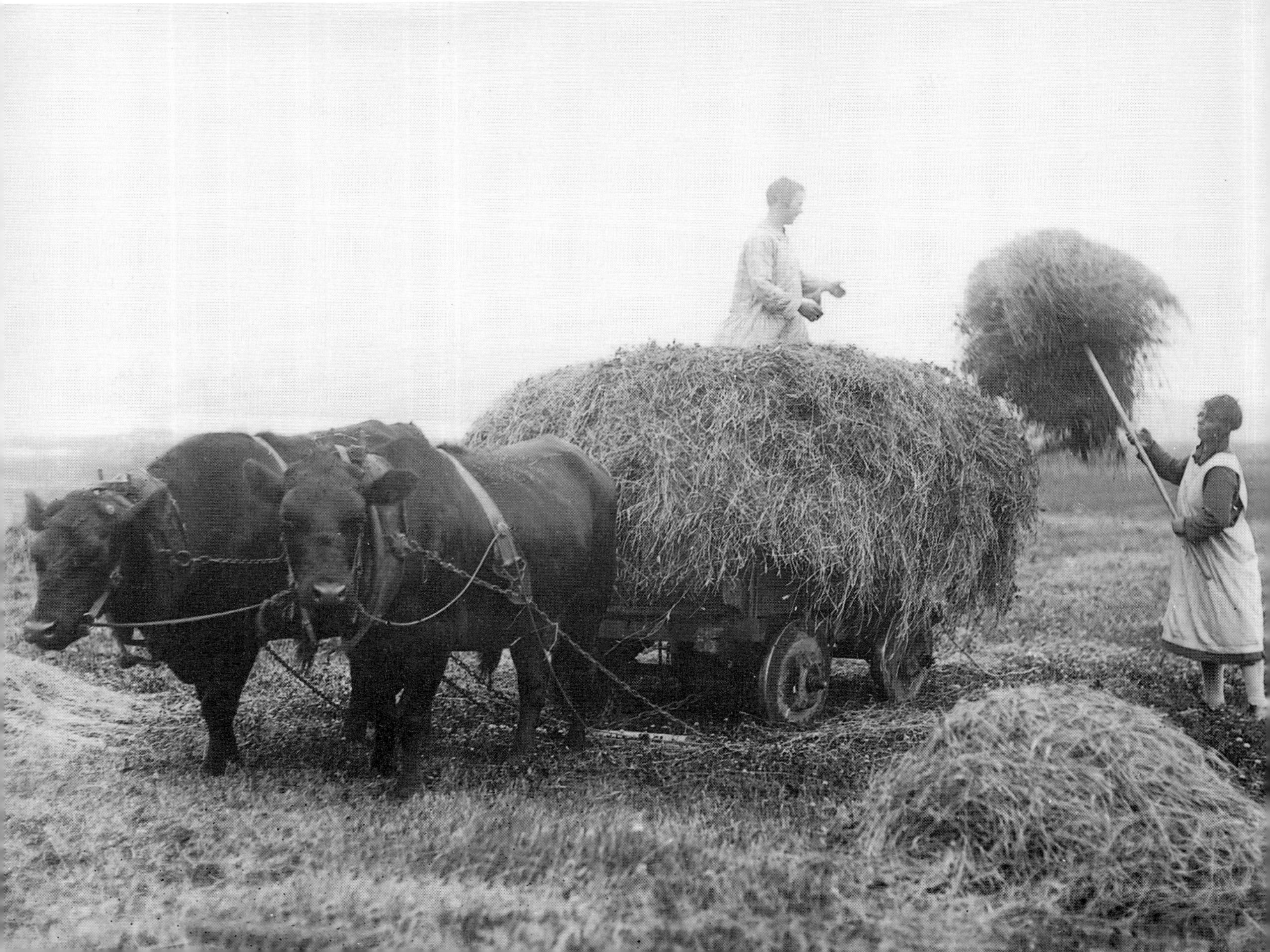

Saving hay, Hoy, Orkneys, 1918

Fascinating reminders of the Norse influence on the Orkneys are to be seen in the ox-drawn solid-wheeled farm cart which these two 'land girls' are loading with dried hay during the last summer of the First World War. Various types of sledge were in use on the Orkneys and on the Scottish mainland at least from Viking times, from the most primitive form, the 'slype', made from a naturally curved and forked wind-bent tree and all in one piece which, according to the late Dr I F Grant, survived almost into this century for the purpose of removing large stones from fields. Except in hilly country with steeply sloping fields where their use continued until the start of this century for bringing in hay, both in Scotland and in the Lake District of England, the more elaborate sledges were replaced by a primitive form of wheeled vehicle, the 'kellach'. These had a single pair of solid wooden wheels, made from three pieces of thick plank, attached to the rear of the vehicle through a turning wooden axle to which the wheels were rigidly fixed. Unlike the wooden wheels in the photograph, the wheels of the kellach did not have metal tyres and wore unevenly, going very quickly out of shape and giving a characteristic wobbling gait and noisy progress to the vehicle.

The four solid wheels of this unusual farm vehicle do not appear to have been rigidly attached to the axle, which is not intended to rotate. They are also seen to be shod with steel tyres. The oxen are smooth-coated and have been de-horned, but notice how they have bits in their mouths as though they were horses. The girls would have been glad of some harvest broth after their work. This soup contains nettles whose nickname, Ivar's Daughter, reminds us again of the Norse influence.

Hairst Bree

1 Kg neck of lamb chops
1 teaspoon salt
1.5L water
4 young turnips, chopped
6 young carrots, sliced lengthwise
2 heaped teaspoons of mint, chopped
1 heaped teaspoon of sugar
6 scallions with the green left on
450g young broad beans
450g young nettle tops
1 young cabbage
1 lettuce-heart, chopped
A large bunch of parsley, chopped
Freshly milled black pepper

Bring the lamb to the boil in the water with the salt and simmer gently for around forty minutes, removing any scum that rises. Gently lift the meat out, de-bone it and remove any lumps of fat, then return it to the stock and add the vegetables, the mint and the sugar. Continue simmering until the vegetables are just cooked – they must not be mushy – then add the chopped parsley, season to taste and serve with hunks of barley bannocks. For barley bannocks (see page 92).

Loading sheep, Orkneys, C. 1920

Even as in the days of the Jarls of Orkney, sheep raising was a major part of the economic life. These young sheep are being moved to another island for fattening and appear to be taking their transportation in a very philosophical spirit, for the rope about the one in the boat is only loosely wound, the others show no sign of alarm and the lamb, in the farmer's arms, looks quite relaxed.

The many boats drawn well up above high-tide level testify to a community as at home in a boat as behind a plough. Traditions from the pagan past still survive on the islands, most noteworthy the three day festival of Up Helly Aa, when a specially constructed Viking ship is burned amidst much celebration and jollity by local men dressed as Norsemen. Kirkwall too, now has a small but important museum of modern art organised by the indefatigable activities of Miss Margaret Gardiner.

It is in these northern regions that barley comes into its own as a staple flour for bread and the bread made from barley is delicious and full of character.

Bere Bannocks

225g barley-meal
50g plain wheat flour
½ teaspoonful of salt
1 level teaspoon sodium bicarbonate
300ml buttermilk or good sour milk
1 level teaspoonful of cream of tartar

A little wheat flour is used in this recipe to make the bannocks easier to shape and handle.

Get your griddle or, failing that, a heavy thick bottomed frying-pan, well heated up so that it is ready for use and smear it with a very little cooking oil before you put the bannocks on it. In a mixing basin mix the barley-meal, wheat flour, salt and cream of tartar well together. Put the bicarbonate into another bowl and pour the buttermilk over it, stirring briskly. When it fizzes pour it at once into the middle of the mixture in the other bowl and work it with your hands into a soft dough. If it seems too dry add a very little more buttermilk. Dredge it with a little more wheat flour and turn it out onto a lightly floured slab and with as little handling as possible. Quickly roll it out until it is about 1cm in thickness and cut into 25cm diameter circles and transfer these to your lightly oiled griddle or pan (a couple of fish slices come in handy for this). Cook steadily but not too quickly until the undersides become brown, then turn them and brown the other sides. To serve attractively, lay them in a dish with a napkin beneath and keep hot until brought to table.

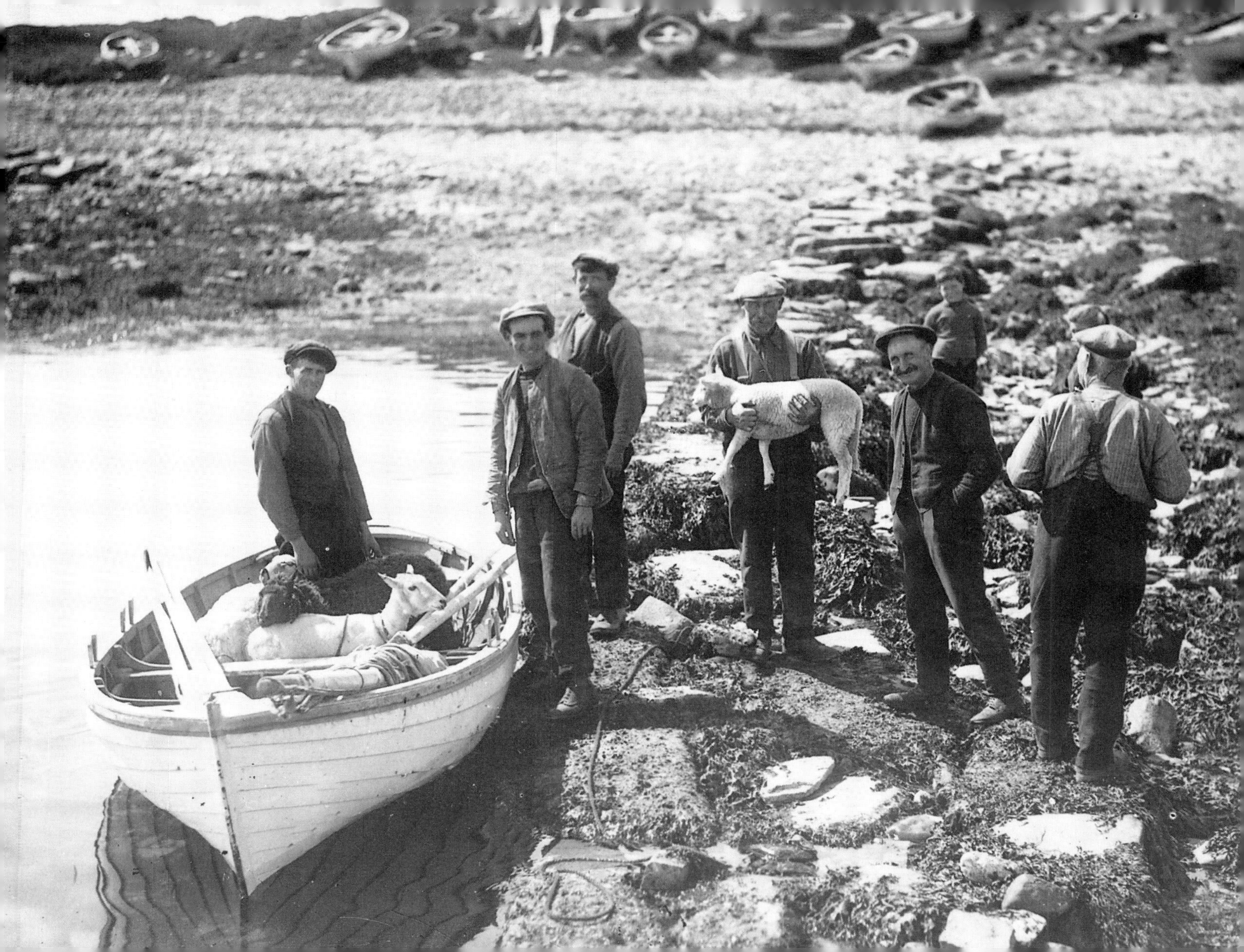

Waiting for duck, Loch nan Clàr, Sutherland, C. 1890

Scotland's many lochs, both salt and fresh water, have always been a favoured resort of sportsmen seeking wild duck, many varieties of which abound. Here a small party of three, or four if the photographer is to be included, together with a well equipped gillie, have settled down on a bank of dry heather by the side of the loch to await the return of the birds. Realising that they may have a long vigil, one is relieved to observe that they appear to have brought a knapsack of provisions with them and the ubiquitous tobacco-pipe which, in those days seems to have been regarded as an essential item for an expedition of this kind.

The young man in the foreground is wearing a kilt and sporran, reminding us that the kilt was a cut-down form of the long plaid. Some have said that the kilt was invented by an English tailor when there was a revival of Celtic dress under the romantic influence of Sir Walter Scott.

The original, long, belted plaid was evolved to cope with the problems of exposure to wet and wind. To put it on, the belt, open, was placed on the ground. The plaid was then folded back and forth in longitudinal folds (the origin of the pleats in the kilt) except for about 30cm at each edge. One then lay down on one's back on the plaid, so that the lower edge of the plaid came to just above one's knees, overlapped the unfolded edges across one's front, fastened the belt around one's waist and stood up. The upper part of the plaid, which fell down at the back, could then be manipulated in a number of ways to cover one or both shoulders or to form a kind of tent; a useful garment if sleeping out in the heather. The water-resistant qualities of the wool in the old tweeds enabled a novel way of keeping warm to be employed. Having made oneself a small form in the heather so that the plants afforded shelter from the direct effect of the wind, one soaked one's plaid in a burn, wrung it out well and wrapped oneself in it and lay down in one's form. Soon one's body heat had formed a layer of water vapour around one which, because of the high latent heat of water, served to diminish direct heat radiation and actually helped to keep one warm, so that with a plentiful supply of water-soaked oatmeal to keep up one's calories, one was in a much better state than a conventionally dressed soldier of the eighteenth century. It would be of little use to seek to use a kilt in this fashion, ornamental and attractive though they are. Curiously, there is only one gun to be seen, so perhaps the party is more interested in wild life than in shooting.

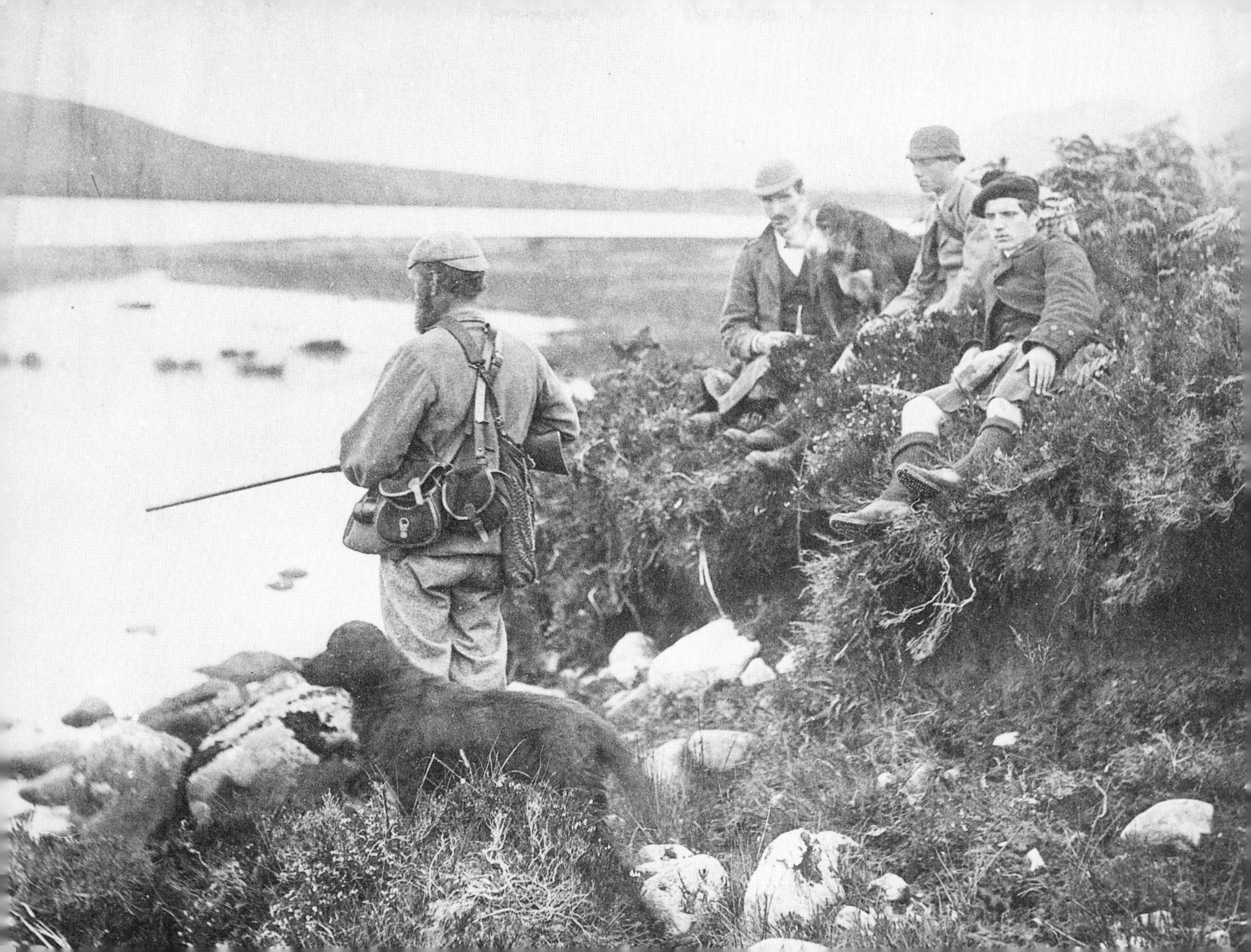

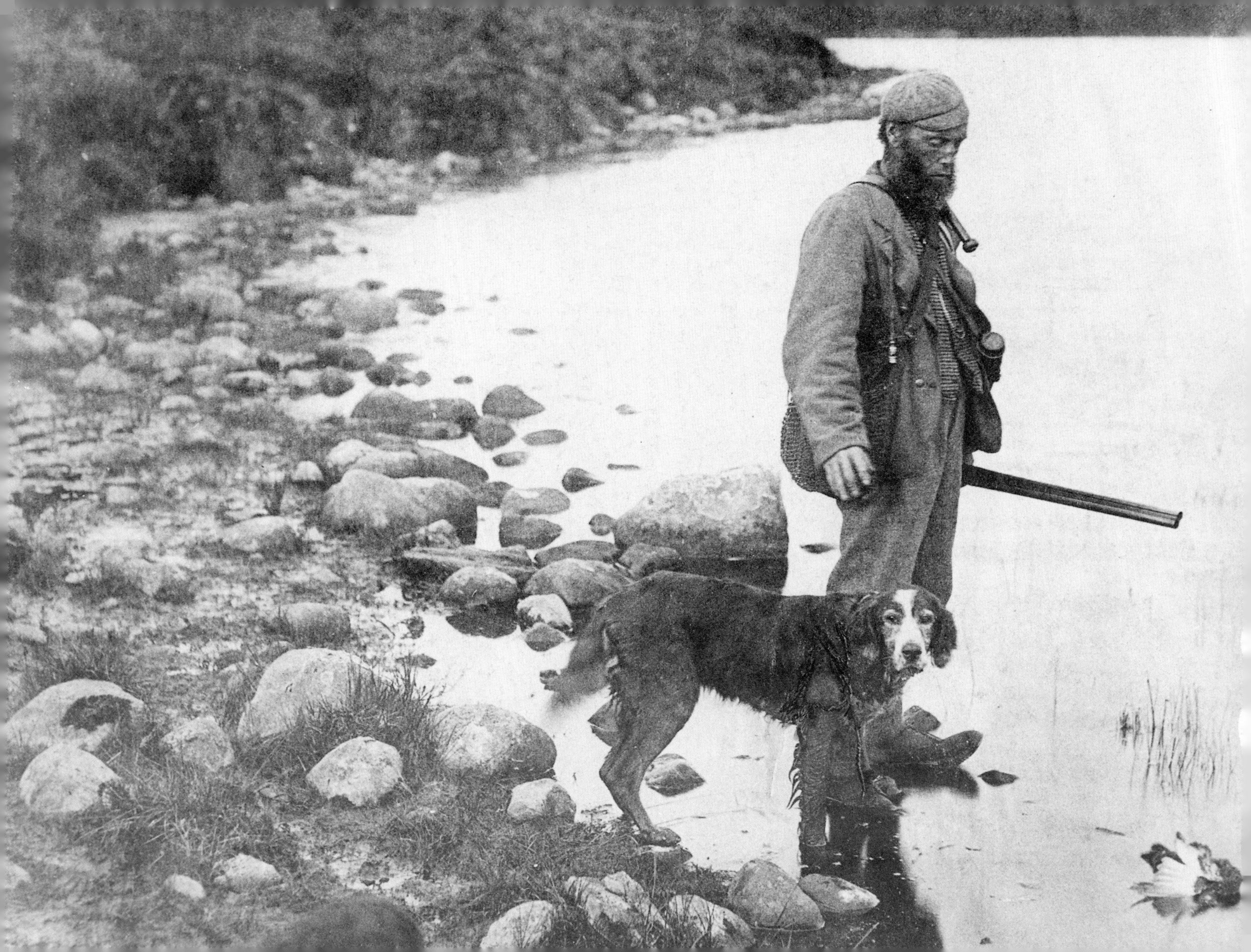

The gillie bags a snipe, Sutherland, C. 1890

WHATEVER THE STATE OF THE REST OF THE PARTY, THE GILLIE IS seriously equipped for his work, with his game-bag and pouches for cartridges, telescope, whistle and dogs as well as capacious pockets in his jacket and trousers, for which a sporran would be a poor substitute, and he appears to have brought down a snipe, though one of his dogs seems more interested in the photographer than in the game, leading one to the suspicion that the bird may be 'salted', like Antony's fish.

All varieties of snipe should be skinned, never plucked and when immediately freshly shot may be grilled and eaten. Remove the crop but do not draw the birds, for the traill is a delicacy.

Roast the birds on a spit in front of a peat fire, when you will find them to be perfectly tender.

When roasted, scoop out the traill and serve it on a slice of toast with each bird. Like woodcock, the brains are delicious and should not be overlooked. Woodcock may be treated in exactly the same way and a peat fire makes an ideal grill with just the correct wavelengths of heat emitted if the body of the fire is large enough. The peat smoke contributes its delicious piquancy, but do not over expose the birds to it.

Children by the river, Inverness, C. 1900

IN ANCIENT TIMES INVERNESS WAS THE CENTRE OF POWER OF THE Picts, to which St Columba came in the year 565, to convert King Brude, and thereby his subjects, to Christianity. The castle in which tradition asserts Macbeth murdered King Duncan once stood in the vicinity but was demolished by Malcolm Canmore who built another castle in its place. Inverness became a royal burg early in the thirteenth century when the Scottish king William the Lion raised it to that dignity and, ever since, it has been regarded as 'the Capital of the Highlands'.

As its name suggests, it was also an important city of the Vikings, to whom a town situated on sheltered waters would appeal as a natural prize.

In the distance is Inverness Castle, the seat of Local Government offices and the Law Courts. It was built in 1835 to the design of the Scottish architect William Burn.

The boat in which the children are playing was used to set a large net in the river to catch salmon, the net being then drawn in by the transportable geared winding mechanism at the right of the photograph. Parts of the seine and its floats can be seen in the water astern of the boat and the children are obviously gathering to watch the salmon netting. They are going to be pretty tired when they get home, but the mothers of some of them may perhaps have made them that splendid old Scottish toffee known as 'glessie'.

Glessie

1 teaspoon of cream of tartar
15g butter or margarine
2 tablespoons of cold water
700g golden syrup
225g moist Demerara sugar

Put the cream of tartar, sugar, butter and water into a capacious non-stick saucepan with a thick bottom and, stirring continuously, bring slowly to the boil. When all the ingredients are dissolved in the water and it has been boiling steadily for five minutes, add the golden syrup and continue stirring until it comes to the boil again, then boil without stirring for 30 minutes, until a few drops dropped into ice-cold water set into a hard ball. Put it out onto a greased slab and when it has cooled a little, draw a greased knife through its surface to mark it into squares.

When it has become completely cold, place it so that the first rank of squares projects over the edge of a chopping-board and, holding onto the main mass, break it off with a blow from a light hammer. Work in the same way with the strip broken off and you will get satisfactory squares which should be kept in an airtight tin if they are not to become soft and sticky.

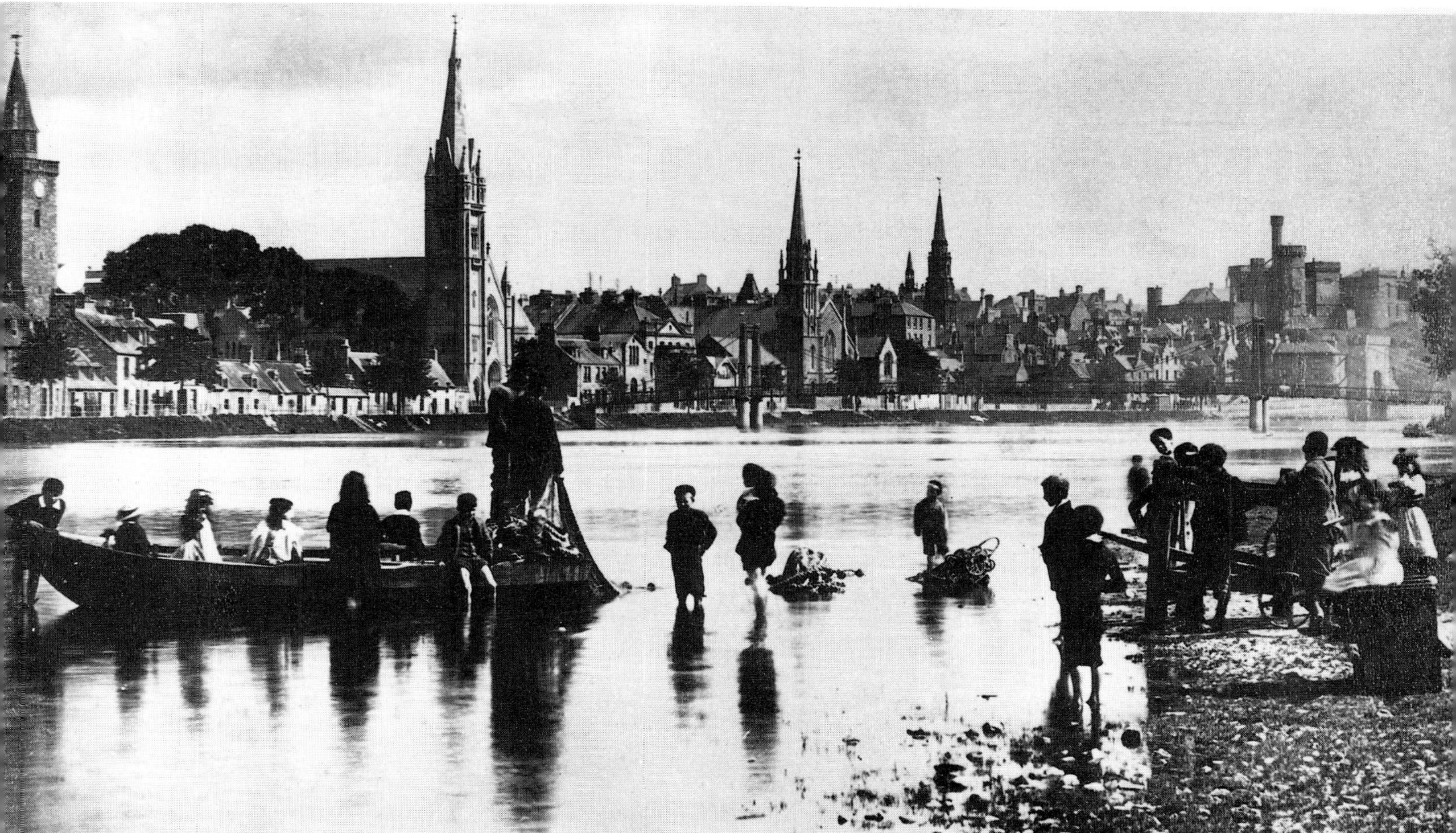

Nannie Shaw's 'Castle', Nairn, C. 1880

THE TRADITION OF THE 'WISE WOMAN' HAS ALWAYS BEEN STRONG in Scottish life and our party would have heard, along the way, many tales of their powers, so that the opportunity to visit one could have been taken as they passed from Inverness to Nairn, where she lived in what she called her 'castle' a little outside the town. Charles Sellar, in his book 'A Glimpse of Old Nairn', 1969, says of her: "Nannie Shaw and her brother Fanny were out-workers (casual farm labourers). They lived in their 'castle' which stood on the Nairn to Inverness road. Nannie had a great reputation as a fortune-teller and many of the youth of that day visited her to have their cups read. Nannie welcomed them as they all brought their small supply of tea with them."

It seems that brother and sister had a reputation for eccentricity and that the local boys were in the habit of playing tricks on them, so Nannie and her brother looked to their security by building the defensive works seen in the photograph.

It is interesting to notice among the debris used to form a barricade to the right of the gate, the partial remains of what appears to have been a 'kellach' (page 91). The three piece wooden wheel and a part of the axle are seen. The 'castle' is a typical 'black house', without windows and built with local materials, wood, peat-divots and reed thatch and although there is what looks like a chimney at the left gable end where a little dry-stone work is seen, the use of this seems to have been abandoned and a simple smoke-hole in the roof suggests that a central stone hearth was in use at the time when this photograph was taken.

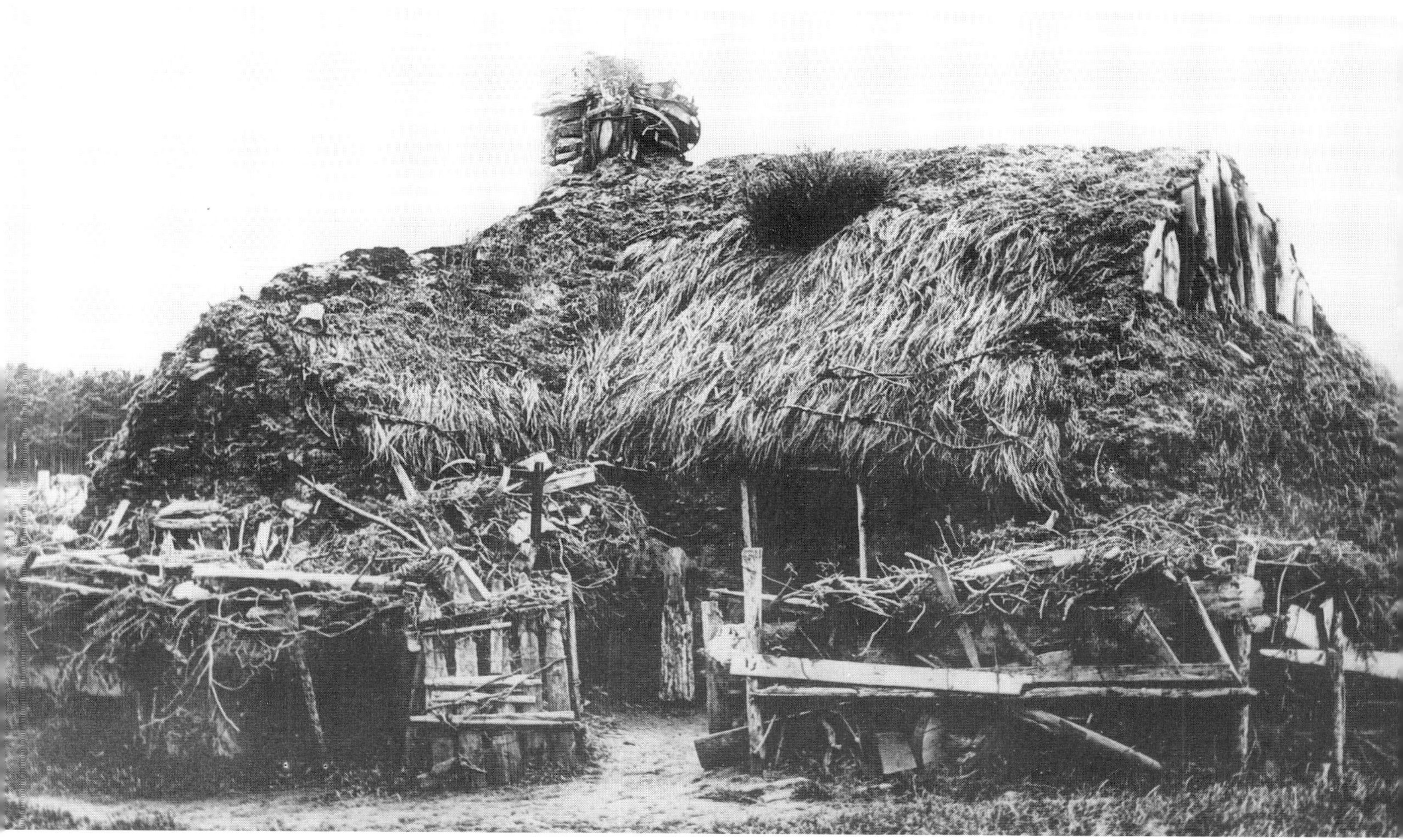

A bedroom in Cawdor Castle, C. 1880

Much confusion exists as to where the murder of King Duncan in 1040 actually took place and many people today entertain the erroneous idea that it happened at Cawdor Castle. The building looks perfect for such a drama, but the truth is that the earliest part of the castle, the keep, was built in 1454 on ground that had no previous building upon it and the part of the building in which this bedroom is situated not until around two centuries later.

Cawdor Castle has been an inspiration to theatrical set-designers, but if we want to imagine what the eleventh century castle, near Inverness, one of the supposed sites of the event, looked like before its destruction by Malcolm Canmore, it would have been closer in appearance to the castle seen in Kurisawa's brilliant adaptation of *Macbeth* called 'Cobweb Castle', which has the incomparable actress Machiko Kyo playing Lady Macbeth in one of the greatest performances of the part this century.

During the season, no visitor to Scotland should depart without having enjoyed the incomparable Red Grouse (*Lagopus scoticus*). They should be hung for a week to ten days, depending on how warm the weather is, before being plucked, drawn and roasted.

Roast Grouse

A brace of grouse (young birds of the year)
2 teaspoons lemon juice
6 slices of fat bacon
Salt and freshly milled black pepper
25g whortleberries or cranberries
150ml good claret, hot
2 grouse livers
2 teaspoons rowanberry jelly (page 60)

Pour half the lemon juice into the body cavity of each bird and wipe round well, then stuff them with the whortleberries or cranberries, swathe the birds completely in the fat bacon, lay them in a roasting-tin and cover the tops of the bacon-wrapped birds with kitchen foil. Pre-heat the oven to 220°C. (425°F.) Gas Mark 7 and when it is hot put the birds in and roast for 20 minutes. Meanwhile fry the grouse livers lightly in a little butter, stopping while the insides of the livers are still pink. Mash them thoroughly, season to taste and spread them on two slices of freshly made toast each of which is large enough to take a bird and reserve the liver-spread toast in a warm oven. After 20 minutes roasting, remove the kitchen foil and the bacon from around the birds, pour the hot claret over them, return them to the oven and roast for 10–15 minutes more, basting often.

Spread the rowanberry jelly on the bacon slices, roll them up and put three on each piece of toast. Make quite sure that the birds do not get overdone and dried. Remove them and mount them on the toasts, keeping them warm while you de-fat the roasting-tin juices in a hot creamer and reduce the de-fatted juices by half in a saucepan on the hob, check for seasoning and serve in a hot sauce-boat with the birds.

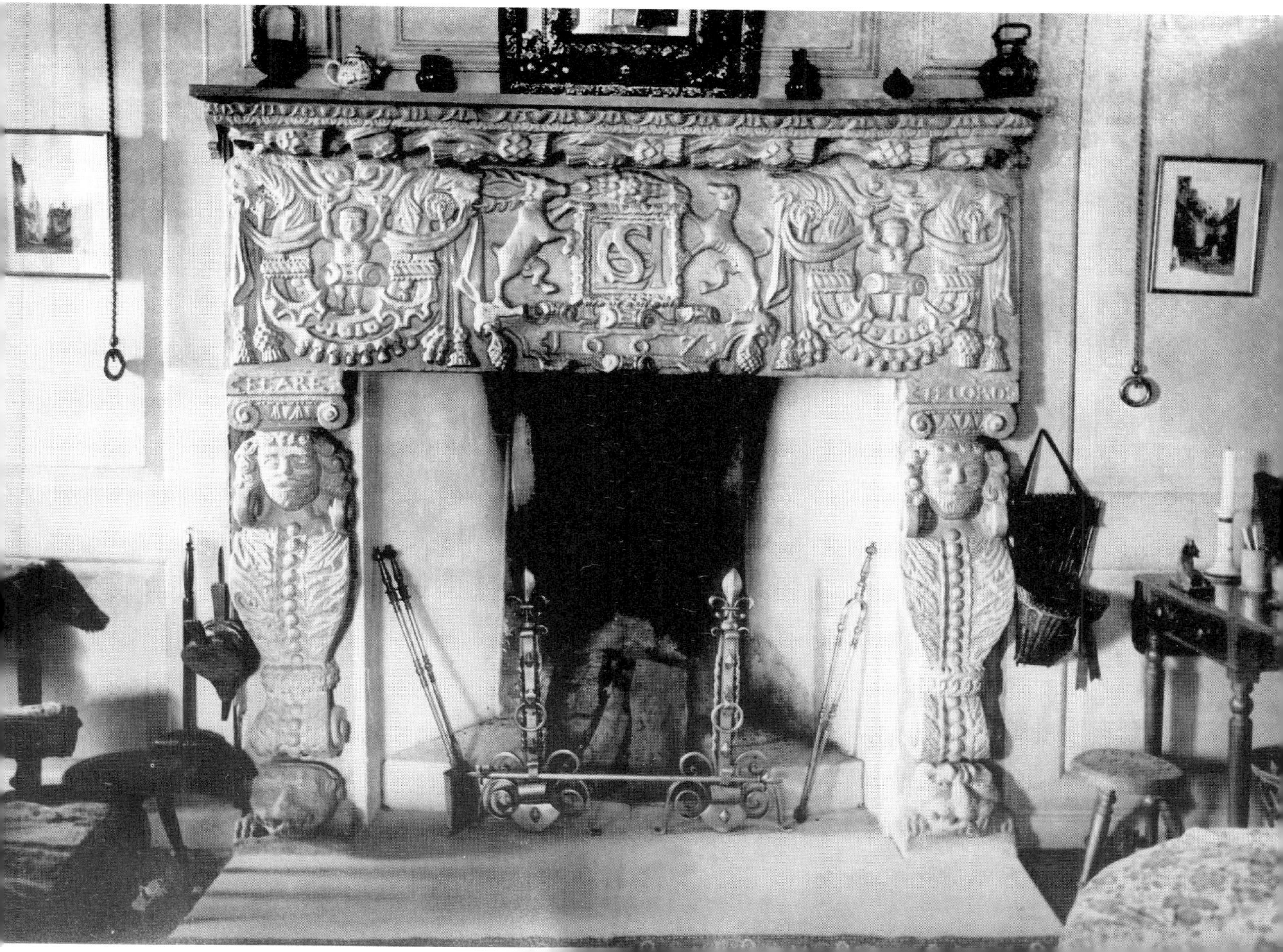
THE LORD

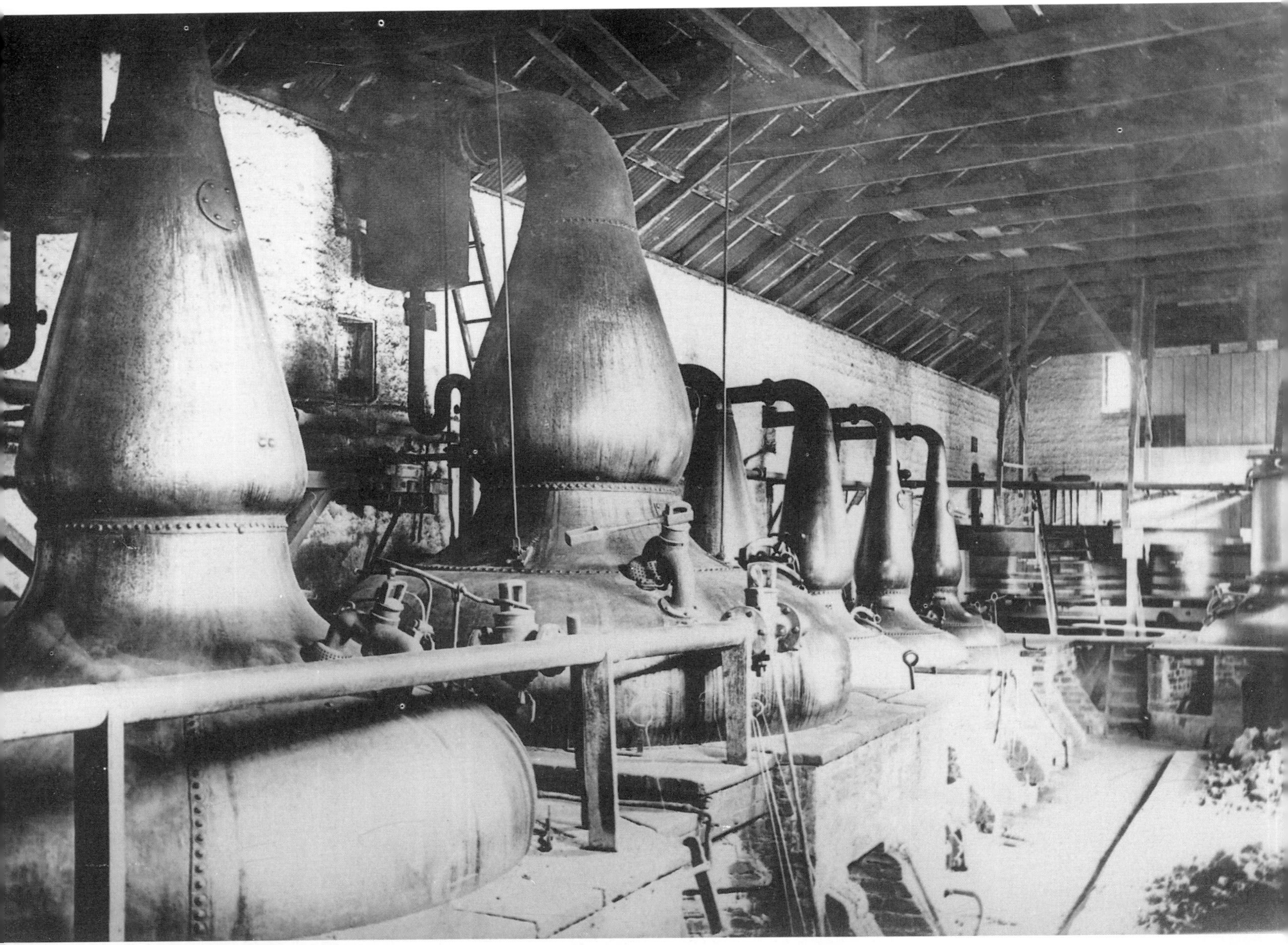

The still-house of a Spey-side Distillery, C. 1880

OF ALL THE DISTILLED DRINKS THE WORLD OVER, THE WHISKIES of Scotland are perhaps the most widely known and most often called for, though the majority who have heard of 'Scotch' may hardly know the great variety and diversity of bouquet and flavour which characterise this great family of spirits. As they made their way towards Aberdeen, our travellers would certainly have been beguiled to visit a Spey-side distillery and, at least some of them might then have been initiated into the delight of savouring a single-malt whisky there. Only one grain, barley, is used in the making of a malt (as distinct from a grain) whisky. The expression 'single' means that the spirit is not a blend of different whiskies but is the product of one distillery. Such whisky takes longer to mature but has great individuality of aroma and taste. The 'peaty' taste that lovers of these whiskies enjoy is introduced in the first stage of the kilning of the malt where peat is used as the kiln fuel so that its smoke, in just the right amount, will flavour the drying malt. This characteristic tang had its historical origin in the fact that the original malt kilns were heated by the nearest available fuel, the peat from the surrounding bogs. In the photograph are seen the copper pot-stills, the form of which resembles the cucurbit and the alembic of the alchemists, the second word reminding us that it was the Arabs who first described the process of distillation.

Barley was converted into malt by being moistened and allowed to sprout in carefully controlled conditions. At just the right moment in its growth it was killed by kilning, ground up and made into a 'mash' with water, then fermented into a 'wort' by the addition of yeast and the wort was then introduced into the largest of the pot-stills, such as that on the left. The output of that still, the 'mash' still, called 'low wines', was introduced into the next still, known as the 'low wines' still and so on, the stills becoming smaller and the spirit more concentrated as the process continued. But distillation is only one, important stage in making a single malt. Years of maturing in oak casks come next. Oak is used as it allows the whisky to 'breathe' so that unwanted products are eliminated by oxidation and after eight, ten or more years the whisky has attained the smoothness, maturity and character of a fine spirit. Only then is it bottled. At first, because it was ready to hand, peat was also used as a fuel to heat the still, but a glance at the still-house floor will show that, even in the 1880s coal had been introduced for that purpose. This is immaterial to the flavour for, once in the still, the flavour of the whisky is unaffected by the smoke of the fuel used for heating.

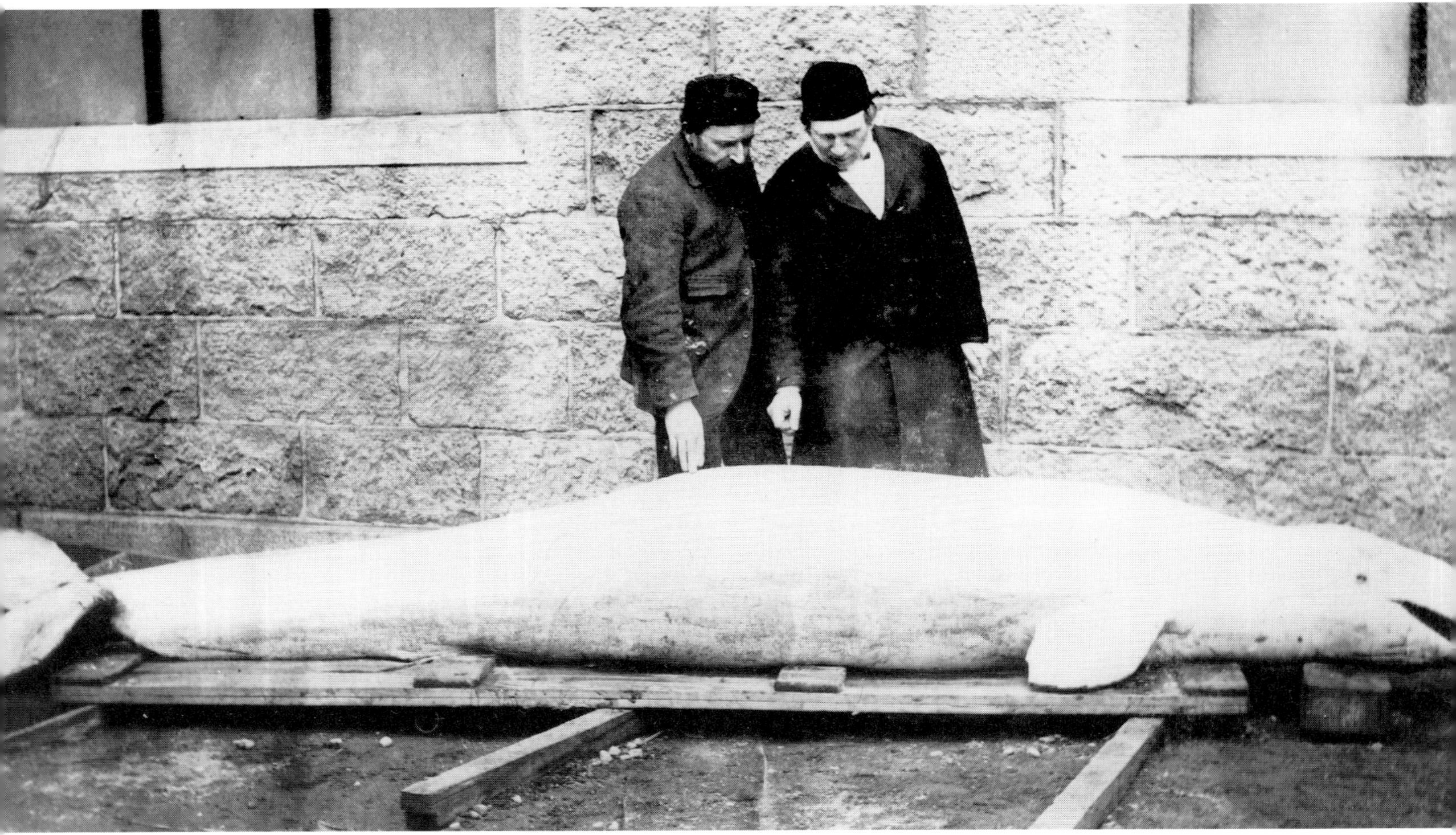

An albino whale undergoing examination at Aberdeen, C. 1885

Though hardly a 'Moby Dick' in point of size, this specimen bears out the occurrence of albinism among whales and so corroborates the veracity of Herman Mellville's great epic novel.

Aberdeen was the centre and heart of the Scottish fishing industry, as it still is today. Until the development of the steam-railway and the steam-trawler, all fishing had to be conducted on a more or less local basis because, in the days before the railways, the internal combustion engine and refrigerated road trucks, it could not be transported in any quantity and at a reasonable price to distant markets before it spoiled. The steam trawlers also enabled more distant fishing-grounds to be exploited and the railways, by providing ice-cooled insulated fish-vans enabled the Scottish east coast fishing ports to supply the large English cities with fresh fish. This development changed the whole balance of the Scottish fishing industry, leading to a decline in fishing from western harbours with the exception of a few centres of which Ullapool became the most important, particularly as a source of herring.

'The Granite City' as Aberdeen is known because of the exceptionally fine locally quarried granite that is used in so many of its buildings, is also a university town and was the centre of the Scottish tea-trade and the port to which so many of the famous tea-clippers made their record-breaking voyages; racing one another home so that the first to arrive would get the best price for their cargoes.

A surgical operation about to be performed without anaesthesia, Aberdeen Royal Infirmary, C. 1875

THIS SINGULAR VISUAL RECORD HAS THE AIR OF HAVING BEEN posed as a demonstration rather than having been a record of an actual procedure. For the 'patient's' sake let us hope so. What a load has been removed from humanity by the development of safe anaesthetic procedures, in the use of which the Scot, Sir James Simpson took a leading part, although his use of chloroform was later, wisely, abandoned. Sir Humphrey Davy, as early as 1800, investigated upon himself the analgesic effects of inhaling nitrous oxide and first suggested its use in surgery.

Of equal importance was the introduction of aseptic techniques. The work of Semmelweiss, Pasteur and Lister laid the foundation for this development, but the conditions under which the operation would appear to be about to take place, as shown in this photograph, might be expected to give a theatre sister of today nightmares for a month. The surgical team are all dressed in their ordinary clothes. The surgeon appears to have just taken his scalpel from his elegant ebony case of surgical instruments on the occasional table to the left and to have gone so far as to turn back his cuffs. His assistants have bared their arms up to the elbow. The furniture of the room has an uncompromisingly domestic look. The operating-table with its turned mahogany legs has had a mattress placed on top on which the patient lies and the small round table on the right of the picture is covered with a cloth with tasselled fringes, thick carpeting and curtains complete the air of domesticity. One can hear our theatre sister shrieking in her sleep!

However, there is one salient indication that times are changing. On the little round table at the right stands a curious piece of apparatus which represents the latest advance in Listerian antiseptic surgical techniques. At its base is a small spirit-burner that raises to boiling point a pressure container of a solution of 1 in 30 parts of carbolic acid in water. In his right hand, the operator of this machine holds a spray nozzle and when the valve is opened a fine spray of carbolic solution is released into the air all around the area of the operation. In these early days it was thought that the application of antiseptic chemicals was the best way of preventing post-operative suppuration rather than the methods in use today of ensuring that the organisms that cause sepsis are excluded. One most interesting feature of this photograph is that there is not a nurse or theatre sister to be seen.

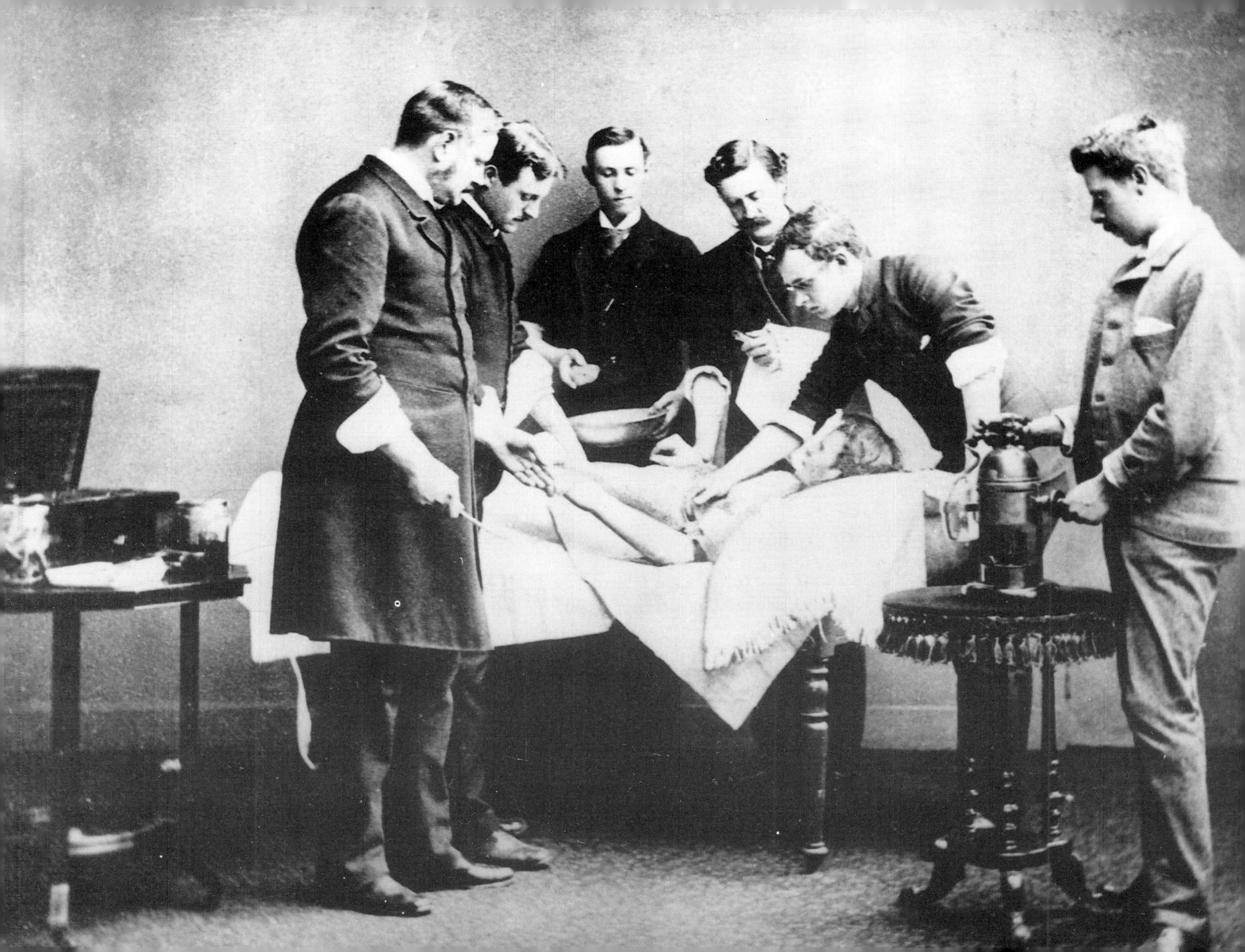

A childrens' surgical ward Aberdeen Royal Infirmary, C. 1888

Around thirteen years later we find a hospital scene that seems more normal to present-day eyes, though here again there are many striking differences. First, one notices that there is no provision for screens around the beds, the small length of curtain behind the surgeon is intended to screen the bed beyond it from draughts from the door. The floors are wooden, with crevices between the boards and the trolleys have that decidedly domestic look that suggests the tea-tray rather than clinical requisites. Clearly, special hospital furniture has not yet begun to be made and installed. The wheelchair at the end of the ward has an antique look with its padded leather and the basin and ewer suggests limited access to hot and cold water. The appearance of a later model of Lister's carbolic spray machine is interesting, for this must be one of the latest models to appear before the apparatus ceased to be used. It reminds us of how important was the introduction of the di-azo derivatives of the mid 1930s such as the two Prontosils and the later family of sulpha drugs which, with the introduction of antibiotics, completely changed the perspectives and practice of surgery. Today, we have to realise that the abuse of these substances on a world scale could return us almost to the nineteenth century through the careless production of resistant strains of micro-organisms.

Aberdeen was also the birth place of Robert Davidson, an early pioneer in the development of electric railway-locomotives whose five ton locomotive, driven by a battery of 40 cells made a number of successful runs on Scottish railways before being sabotaged by employees of the railway who thought the introduction of electric traction would reduce employment. This unhappy incident took place in a locomotive shed at Perth and though the little locomotive had been used effectively for shunting, Davidson's initiative was not followed up. His experiments were carried out before the application of generated power to transportation had been developed.

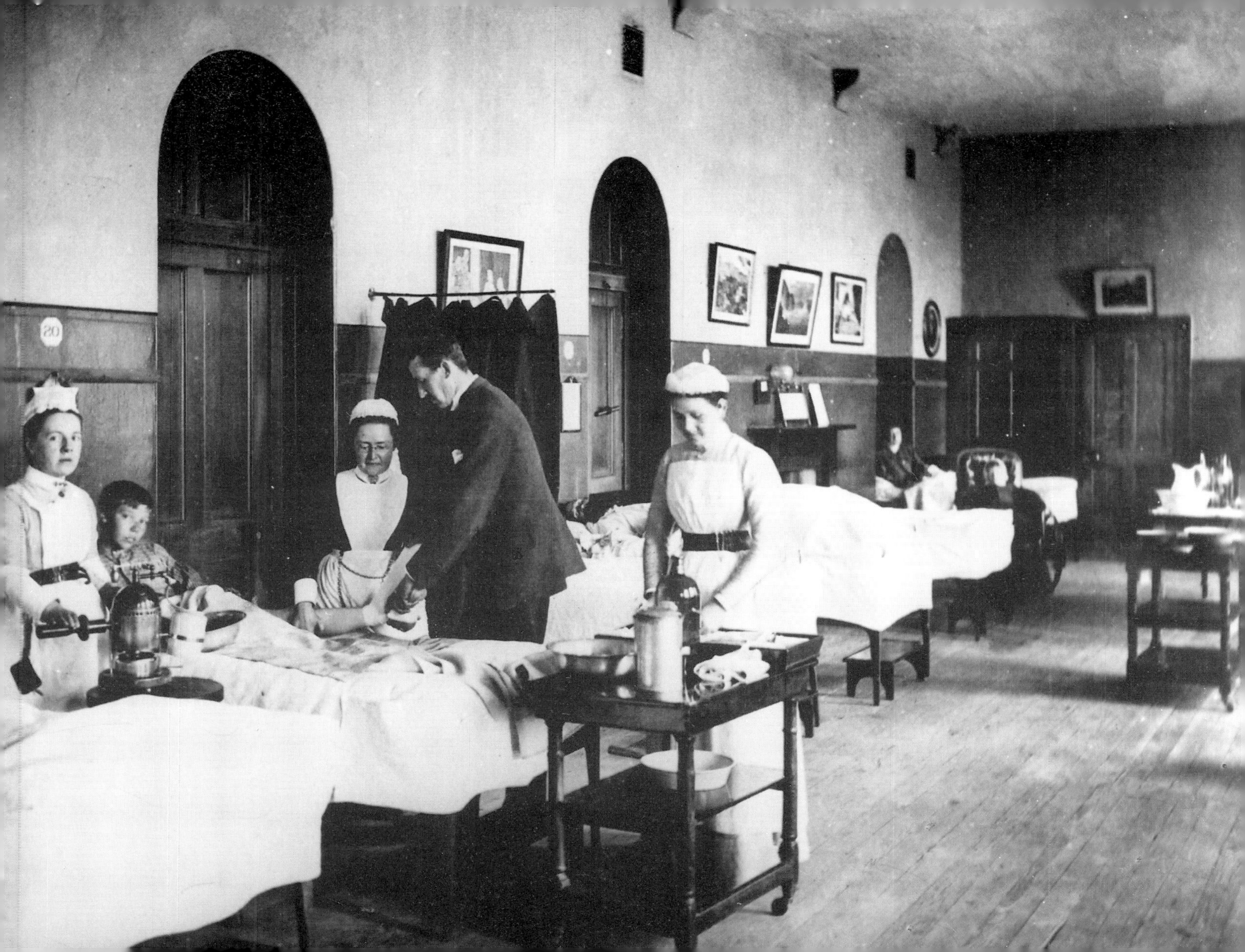

Market Street, Aberdeen, 1890s

This corner of the market is engaged in the coal trade and coal is being weighed, loaded into sacks and the sacks loaded onto carts and horse-lorries for distribution.

The tar-boiler chimney which is seen beyond the horse-lorry reminds us that the roads to which we have become so accustomed were made possible by a Scot: John Loudon McAdam, born in Ayr in 1756. As a schoolboy he made a model road-section and later devoted his life to the study and improvement of roads. Appointed surveyor-general of the Bristol roads in 1815, he introduced the use of tarred lime-stone for road surfacing and thus gave to the world that road surface still called after him, 'macadam'. In 1823, after a parliamentary enquiry into the prevailing methods of road making, McAdam's methods were adopted by local authorities all over the United Kingdom and in 1827 he was appointed general surveyor of roads. Offered, but declining a knighthood, he died at Moffat in 1836. It is indeed difficult to assess the huge extent to which this man's dedication and influence was responsible for accelerating the development of our society.

Aberdeen is famous for its fish market where the bulk of Scottish catches were handled, but it had also made itself known as a centre for confectionery and many varieties of traditional cakes and biscuits are, to this day, still made there. Here is one of the simplest but by no means the least delicious.

Aberdeen Crullas

These small plaited cakes are unusual for they are not baked but fried in deep cooking oil.

125g butter or margarine
½ teaspoon cream of tartar
125g sugar
Pinch of nutmeg
4 eggs, beaten
½ teaspoon salt
450g sifted flour
150ml buttermilk or sour milk
1 teaspoon bicarbonate of soda
Enough cooking oil for deep frying
A little caster sugar for garnishing

Cream the butter and sugar together in a warm bowl, then add the beaten eggs. Thoroughly mix the other dry ingredients together before mixing them also into the creamed butter, sugar and eggs. Add the buttermilk or sour milk gradually, mixing well. Depending on the size of the eggs you may need a little less or a little more buttermilk to achieve a moist but firm dough. When mixed put the dough out onto a floured slab and roll into long strips. Cut these into 25mm wide ribbons, but leaving one end uncut. Plait the ribbons, moistening and pressing together their ends so that they do not come undone. Have the cooking-oil really hot but not smoking and gently lift the crullas into the hot oil with a slice. Fry them until they are just golden, drain them on a bed of kitchen paper, cool them on a wire rack and dust them with caster sugar when they are quite cold. Store in an airtight tin.

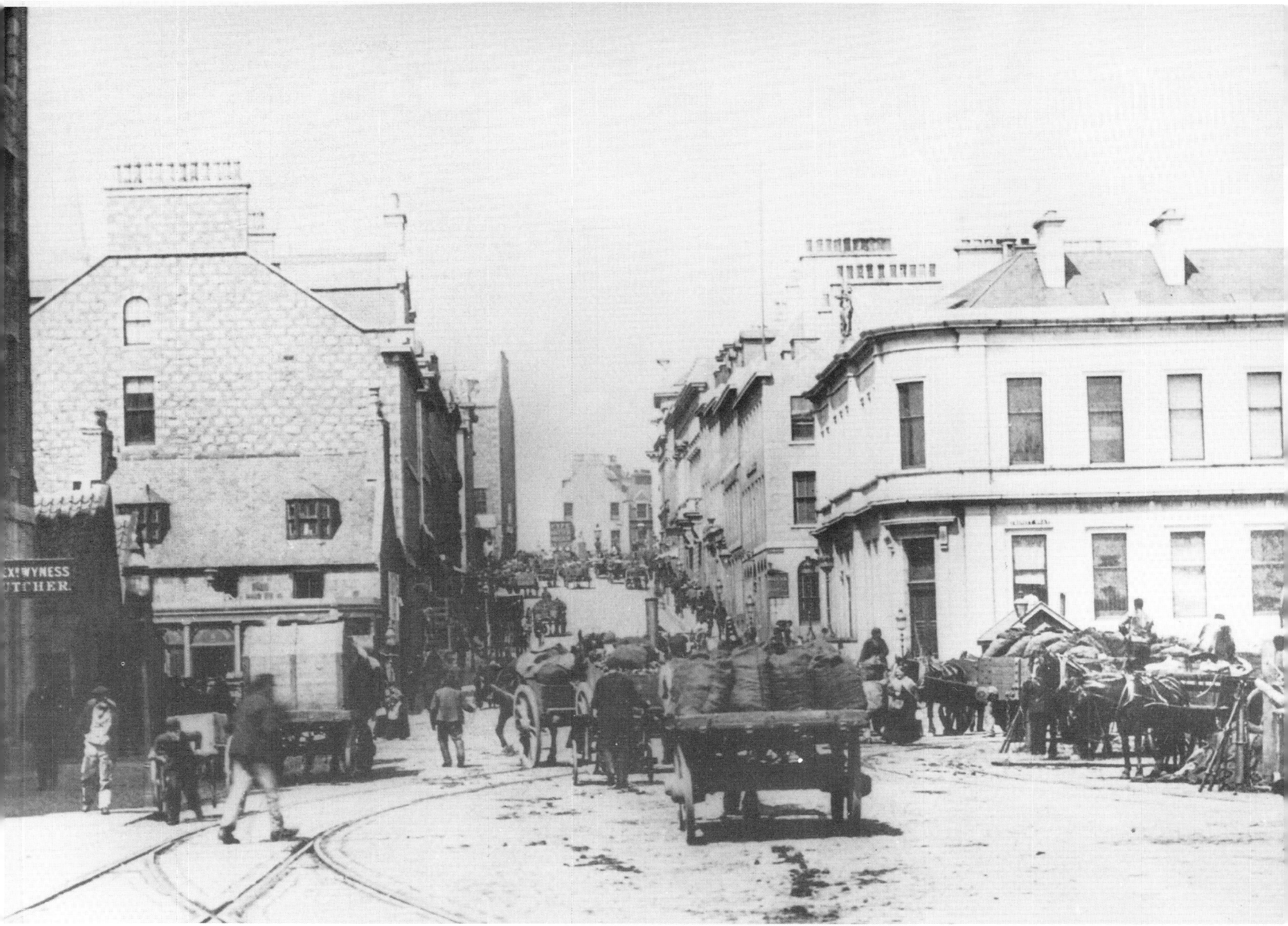

EX. WYNESS
UTCHER.

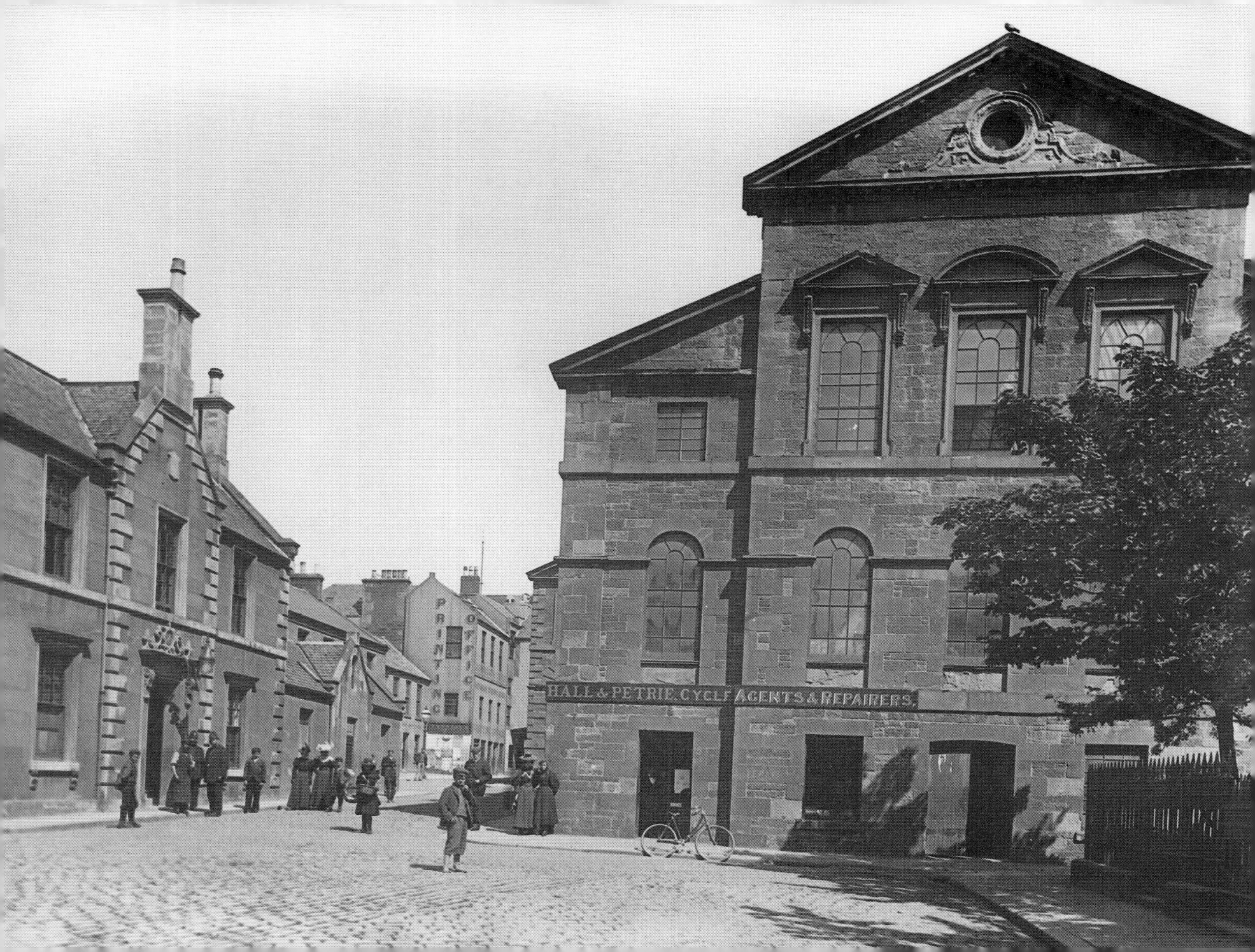
HALL & PETRIE, CYCLE AGENTS & REPAIRERS,
PRINTING OFFICE

The Post-Office and the Market Hall, Arbroath, 1897

As they made their way towards Edinburgh along Scotland's east coast our travellers would have come to the historic town of Arbroath or, as its name was in former times, Aberbrothock (The Mouth of the Brothock), from the river, called after an early saint, that flows into the sea there.

Up to the time of the Dissolution, one of Scotland's greatest abbeys stood here and the stone-work of its fine rose-window is still to be seen today. The town was created a royal burg in 1186 and in 1320 a parliament that supported Robert the Bruce was held here. The town still has the charter which it was granted in 1599.

A mile north, at the old church of St Vigeans is to be found one of the most interesting ancient monuments of Scotland, a stone bearing a Pictish inscription in runes.

But the fame of this town does not rest alone on historical monuments for here is produced a monument of the gastronomical art, a delicacy so unique that it may hold its own as one of the finest forms of smoked fish in the world.

Anyone who has never tasted an Arbroath Smokie has never experienced the most light, subtle and delicious form that a haddock can assume in any guise. The secret lies in the way in which this otherwise fairly ordinary fish is prepared. Originally this used to be done at the nearby village of Auchmithie but Arbroath became the centre of production nearly two centuries ago and this is how they are made. Small haddock, cleaned but not split or rizzarded, are tied by the tails in pairs and hung over a specially prepared fire, the fuel of which is composed of a mixture of oak and birch chips. To prevent the smoke from reaching the fish too directly a number of halved whisky barrels are placed between the fish and the fire to act as a diffusing screen.

The smokies should be gently heated in a low oven, then split and the backbone removed. They should then be very lightly dusted with freshly ground black pepper, dotted with a little butter, closed again and heated once more.

It is important that they are not allowed to dry up but should be served as soon as they are brought up to heat again. It seems an absolute shame that this most delicious variety of smoked fish is so very difficult to get hold of outside Scotland. Taste it while you are there and you will ever after long for more.

Intersection of High Street and Methven Street, Perth, C. 1900

This is one of the comparatively few towns of Scotland to have been a town in Roman times, when its Roman name was Victoria. It was occupied by the Romans for 350 years, but after their withdrawal it reverted to its earlier Gallic name of Aber Tha, The Mouth of the Tay. Aber Tha became changed in time to Bertha, which, still later, became Perth.

It was a centre of Pictish culture and after St Columba's visit, during which he converted the inhabitants to Christianity, the original church, dedicated to St John the Baptist was built. This was much enlarged in the thirteenth and fifteenth centuries and restored in 1891. It was in this church, in 1559, that John Knox preached his famous sermon against idolatry. The first capital of the Kings of Scotland was in Scone where they were by custom crowned upon the *Lia Fail* or 'Stone of Scone' as it was also called. This coronation stone was lent by the Scots to the Irish for a coronation and unfortunately not returned, being later seized by an English monarch. It has now been returned to Scotland and can be seen at Edinburgh Castle. The Scottish kings continued to be crowned at Scone until 1437.

The town had become a burg in 1106 and was made a royal burg in 1210 by the Scottish king, William the Lion. It became the royal capital after the abandonment of Scone and the historic Treaty of Perth, which brought to an end the long war between Scotland and Norway and secured the cession to Scotland of the Hebrides and the Isle of Man, was signed here in 1268.

Many of the Scottish parliaments were held in Perth and it remained the capital of Scotland until this was moved to Edinburgh for the coronation of King James II in 1437 as a consequence of the murder of James I in the Blackfriars monastery in Perth in the previous year.

Much detail of its early history has been difficult to recover as the town records were removed by the English king, Edward I. It had an important salmon fishery on the Tay from early times which is still of economic importance and the development of the dyeing industry by the world famous Pullars of Perth was an important source of employment in the town.

In a house in Curfew Row, still standing today, lived Catherine Glover, the 'Fair Maid of Perth', the heroine of Sir Walter Scott's romance of clan warfare of that name, which later was the inspiration of the libretto of a world famous opera.

In a rather unusual situation, the North British Railway, the Caledonian Railway and the Highland Railway all shared the use of the town station, which must have been found convenient by the inhabitants as well perhaps as by our travelling party now on their way to Edinburgh.

TEETH
SINGLE TOOTH FROM 2/6
CAMERO
LIMITED
SOUTH METHVEN STREET
TOBACCO

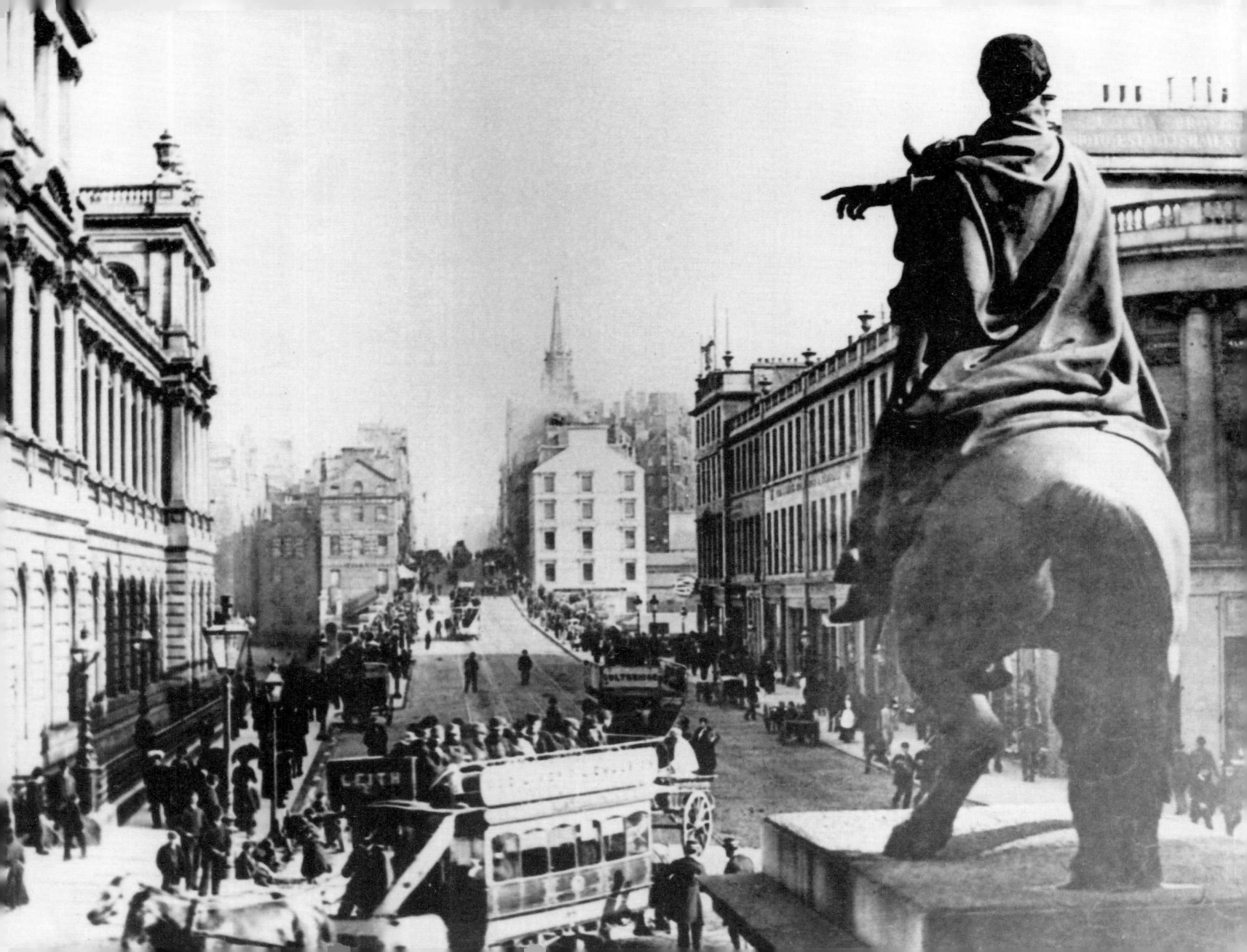
LEITH

Looking from the Register Office, south down North Bridge, C. 1870

LIKE ROME, EDINBURGH HAS BEEN BUILT ON A NUMBER OF HILLS and on the low-lying land between them. Before the coming of the Romans, the area between the river Tyne and the Firth of Forth was occupied by a Brythonic tribe, the Ottadeni, an off-shoot of the Brigantes. They are thought to have built the first fortification on the top of Edinburgh Rock. After the Roman occupation of three and a half centuries, the Southern Picts displaced the Ottadeni, occupying the fort and the surrounding settlements which began the accretion which was later to form the city of Edinburgh. The Picts were in turn ousted, in 617, by the Saxons under Edmond, king of Northumbria, from whom the city takes its name, its Saxon form being given as 'Edwinesburch' by Symeon of Durham in 854.

James the Second was the first Scottish king to be crowned in Edinburgh and he took up residence in Holyrood Abbey, where later was built the palace of Holyrood House. He made Edinburgh the premier royal burg of Scotland in his Royal Charter of 1452 and several later royal charters increased its privileges. During the religiously and politically active sixteenth century, Edinburgh took a leading part in events, but after the signing of the Act of Union in 1703, which took place hidden from the light of day in the cellar of a house in High Street, the life of the city declined as did that of Dublin, after a similar event a century later.

More than fifty years were to elapse before returning growth was seen. The first North Bridge was constructed in 1763, but, by the end of the eighteenth century, the New Town, as planned by the distinguished Scottish architect James Craig, was nearly complete.

Across the bridge, on the right of the street is seen the spire of Christ Church at the Tron, which dates from 1637, as did its companion edifice in Glasgow, both taking their popular name from their proximity to the tron or beam-balance where the merchants' weights were verified. If any merchant or shopkeeper had weights which were found to be below standard, it was the custom of the times to nail him by his ears to the beam, an unpleasant, but probably effective way of securing uniformity of measure. Happily the Edinburgh Tron Church has survived to us intact and its bells ring in the New Year to the assembled crowds of celebrating Edinburgh citizens.

The North and South Bridges, such a characteristic feature of Edinburgh, were necessary to bridge the two parallel valleys containing little lochs, now drained. The northern of these narrow valleys was cleverly used to bring the railway through the town without it having to appear overhead or disrupt traffic at street level and the greatly expanded Waverley Station and marshalling-yard now occupies the site of the drained Nor' Loch.

NORTH BRITISH STATION HOTEL

EAST COAST RAILWAY COMPANIES
MIDLAND RAILWAY

COOK'S
TOURIST OFFICE

New Route to ENGLAND

COOK'S
TOURIST
OFFICE

DUNLOP, HATTER

North British Railway Company's Hotel and Thomas Cook's tourist office, Edinburgh, C. 1880

It is not only through being the capital of Scotland that Edinburgh has laid claim to the interest of travellers, then, as now. It has been for the last three hundred years a centre of culture, particularly in the literary field, a centre both of writers and publishers, the marked effect of which is brought to mind at once when we consider the widespread influence of the Edinburgh Review and Blackwoods Magazine, an influence which was felt by the most distinguished writers of their times as Lord Byron's *English Bards and Scots Reviewers* makes us recall. The literary ethos of Edinburgh has always been able to hold its own with that of any city in these islands and this is today greatly enhanced by its Festival which stakes a world-wide claim for serious attention. The Festival has become one of the most culturally recreative events to be found anywhere in Europe and has greatly stimulated tourism.

The photograph shows us a most effective and ingenious example of town-planning. The narrow valley through which the railway was led through the city was, in large areas, covered over to allow recreational areas to be developed on the top of other municipal facilities such as assembly rooms, markets and the ever-growing Waverley Station of the North British Railway Company whose hotel is seen at the left. A quite modest looking establishment in the 1880s it grew to be one of the finest hotels in the city by the turn of the century. In the window of the Railways Office on the ground floor is seen an advertisement for the newly arrived 'sleeping-cars'.

Just to the right is Thomas Cook's tourist office, reminding us of how the collaboration of the Scottish railways assisted the rapid development of his firm in its early days, though this link had been severed by the time that this photograph had been taken. He had developed so much overseas touring that his business was in full expansion.

Right up to the start of the First World War, the wearing of hats was *de rigeur* for both sexes and the tall, silk hat an essential for most social occasions. The manufacturing of these called for a very high glossy finish and required the use of mercury, so that some hatters of the last century were prone to suffer from chronic mercury poisoning, before the risks of absorption were fully understood. It was the symptoms of this condition that led to the common expression 'mad as a hatter' and to that engaging character found in *Alice in Wonderland*.

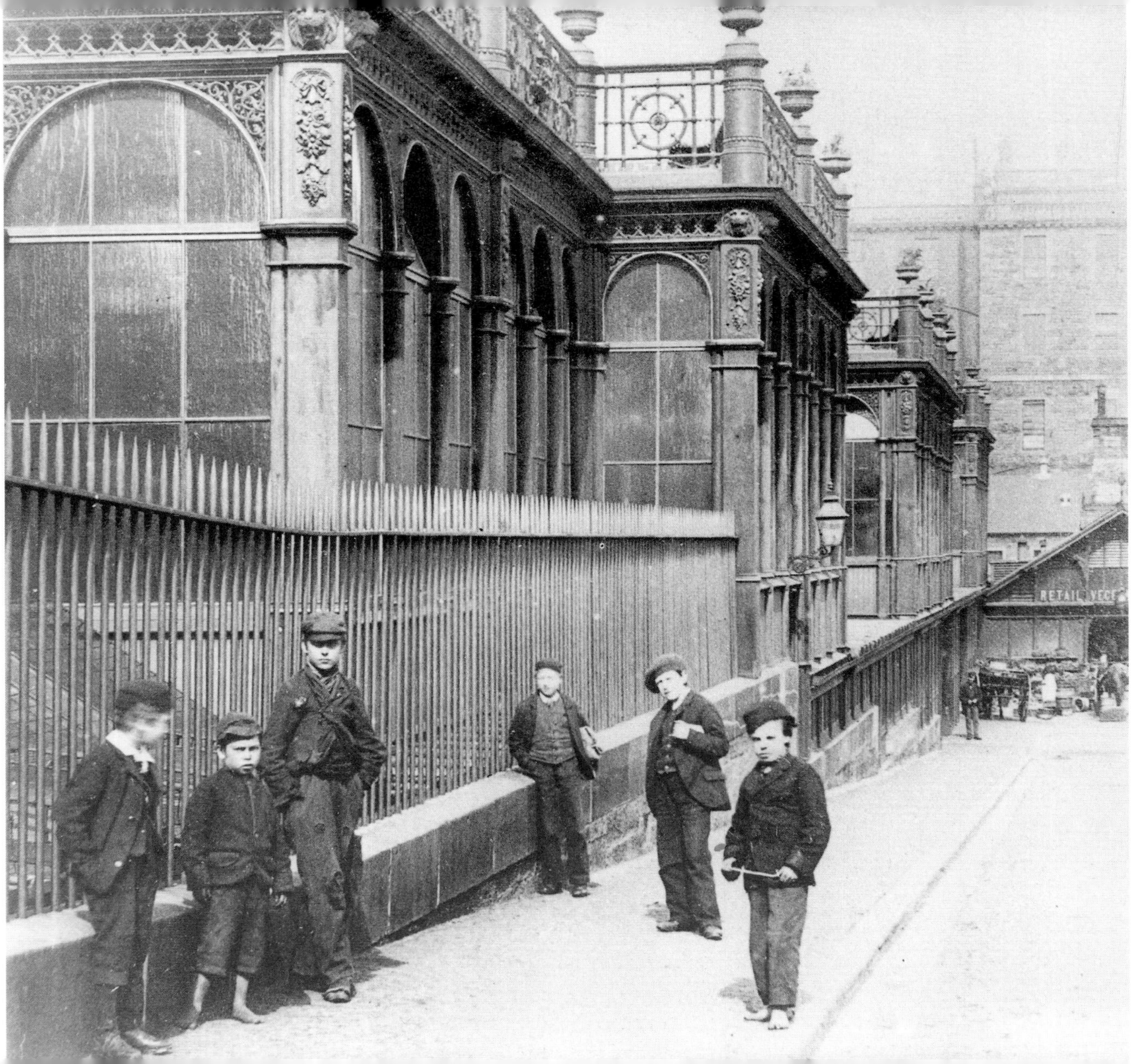
RETAIL

Young Edinburgh boys, C. 1880

BEFORE THEY TAKE LEAVE OF THE CAPITAL CITY OF SCOTLAND OUR travellers will have been sure to visit the house where the great religious reformer John Knox lived and where some of his furniture is still to be seen today. As they made their way to Waverley Station at the end of their circular tour they would have seen more of the ingenious use of the narrow valley made by the Edinburgh town-planners of the nineteenth century. Beneath the gardens are assembly rooms and beneath all the station itself and beside it is the vegetable market where the produce may be expeditiously supplied from the railway. Few cities of the British Isles had at this time such a rational, functional city centre complex in which the hampering irregularity of the ground was exploited to such advantage. It is interesting to notice that the market sold vegetables retail as well as wholesale. Like Glasgow, Edinburgh had at this time terrible slums, the clearance and redevelopment of which took a great many years. Edinburgh was more successful than Glasgow in retaining its ancient buildings and we have a better picture today of what sixteenth and seventeenth century Edinburgh looked like than we do of Glasgow in those times.

It is plain that these six boys, two of whom have no shoes, come from one of the slum areas of the city and are hanging around the railway station and vegetable market area in the hope of picking up some casual work, as the one delivering a package appears to have done. Let us hope that, to keep up their energy they might have about them, in a dusty pocket, some of that delicious traditional form of toffee known as taiblet.

Taiblet

225g butter or margarine
450g sweetened condensed milk
0.5L water
1.8kg caster sugar
A few drops of vanilla essence

Put the butter and water into a capacious non-stick saucepan and put on a low heat, stirring with a wooden spoon until the butter is melted, then add the sugar and bring to the boil, stirring continuously so that the sugar will not catch and burn. When it reaches a steady boil and all the sugar is dissolved, add the sweetened condensed milk and simmer for 20 minutes more, stirring continuously to prevent sticking, then remove from the heat and beat energetically for 5 minutes, adding a few drops of the vanilla essence. Pour into a greased tin, allow it to cool a little and then divide it into bars of a convenient size. When completely cooled, wrap each bar in greaseproof paper and store in an airtight tin.

Train arriving at Berwick-on-Tweed Station, 1901

Having passed southward-bound across the Tweed, the Scottish part of our travellers' expedition was over. The return by rail along the East Coast Route is not nearly so picturesque and revealing as the approach from the sea up the Clyde. A refreshments trolley is ready on the platform for the train seen in the photograph is only a local one and without a restaurant-car, though it is interesting to see that the locomotive, even as late as the date of the photograph, has no roof to its driver's cab, merely a spectacle-plate; this shows the durability of some of these elderly engines of an earlier epoch.

Those of our travellers who were heading for London would have completed their journey on an express which would have had full restaurant service on board. For many years, and until at least only a few years ago, the kitchen-car staffs changed at Berwick-on-Tweed. On the south-bound trains the Scottish chef was replaced by an English one and vice-versa. After passing northward over the Tweed one experienced, at the very next meal, a subtle change in the character and presentation of the food. The veritable savour of Scotland.

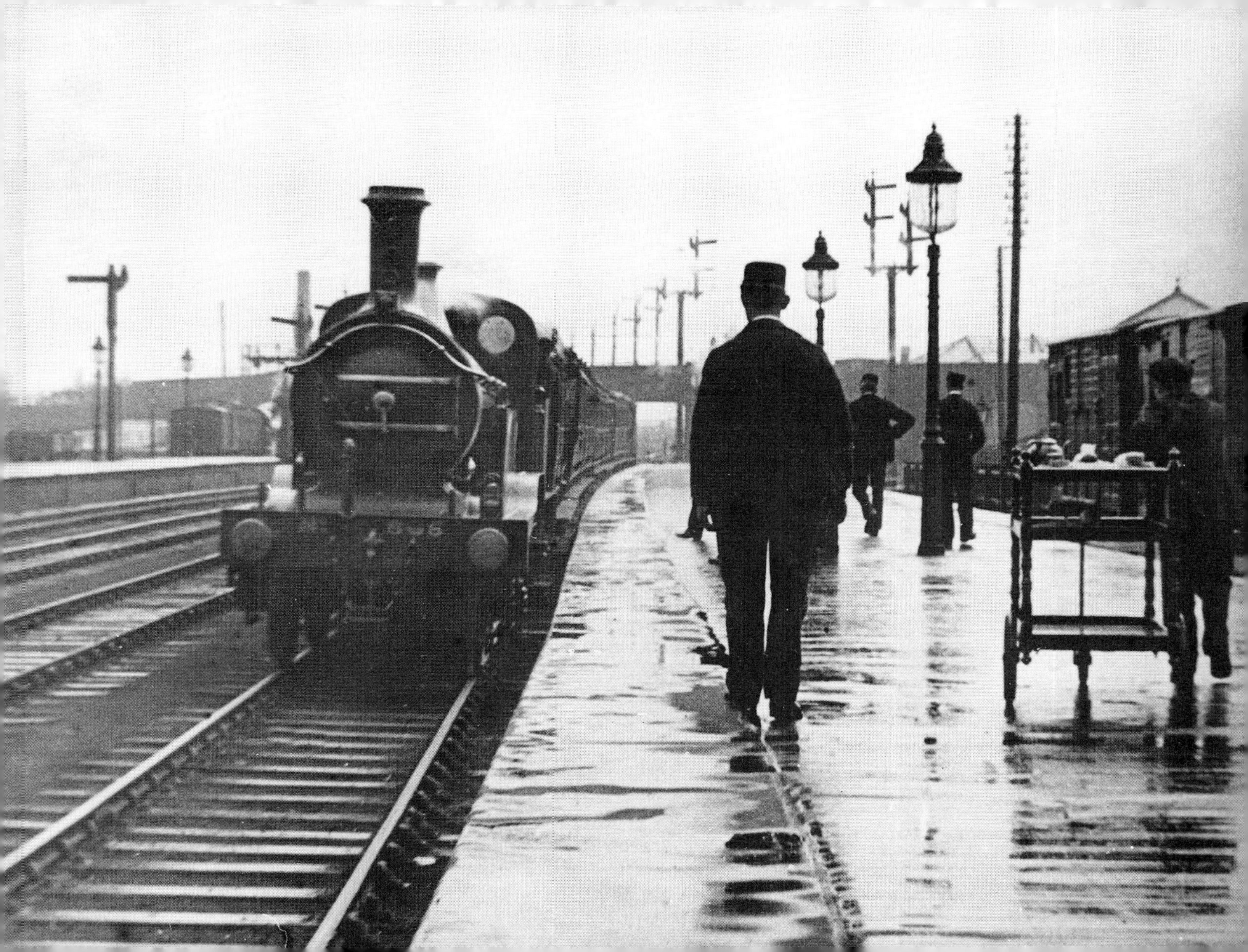